# Positive Behavior Support
# Training Curriculum
# 3$^{rd}$ Edition

> Trainee
> Resource Guide

by
Dennis H. Reid, Marsha B. Parsons, and David A. Rotholz

American Association on Intellectual and
Developmental Disabilities

*Published by*
American Association on Intellectual and Developmental Disabilities
501 Third Street, NW, Suite 200
Washington, DC 20001

*To order*
AAIDD Order Fulfillment
501 Third Street, NW, Suite 200
Washington, DC 20001
Phone: 202-387-1968 x216
Email: books@aaidd.org
Online: http://aaidd.org/publications/bookstore-home

Product No. 4161
ISBN 978-0-9965068-3-0

Printed in the United States of America

# Acknowledgments

This curriculum was originally developed, validated, and implemented on a statewide basis by the South Carolina Department of Disabilities and Special Needs (SC DDSN). Throughout all editions of the curriculum its development and implementation were conducted by Habilitative Management Consultants, Inc., The University of South Carolina Center for Disability Resources (UCEDD), and the SC DDSN. The authorship of the curriculum reflects the contributions of those who translated SC DDSN's intentions into a meaningful, practical, and evidence-based training curriculum.

We gratefully acknowledge the important contributions of Bruce Braswell and LouAnn Morris to the earlier editions of this curriculum and to the lasting impact of their efforts. We similarly acknowledge the multiple contributions of Dr. Carolyn Green and their positive impact on this edition of the curriculum.

# Contents

## Modules for Direct Support Staff and Supervisory Trainees

## Modules for Supervisory Trainees

# Module 1: Dignity and Behavior Support

**Objectives:**                                                    **Trainee Notes**

Upon completion of this module, trainees should be able to:

(1) Identify at least two goals of Positive Behavior Support
(2) Identify at least two values of Positive Behavior Support
(3) Describe the Antecedent, Behavior, Consequence (ABC) Model

## Introduction to Positive Behavior Support

In this and the classes to follow, we will be talking about positive behavior support. When people think about positive behavior support, they often think about working with behavior problems. Helping people overcome problem behavior *is* a major goal of positive behavior support. However, positive behavior support has other important goals as well.

---

### Goals of Positive Behavior Support

*to support people with disabilities to:*

1. Enjoy life

2. Be as independent as possible

3. Have a normal life

4. Overcome problem behavior

---

1

One goal is to help people with disabilities enjoy their lives. Another goal is to support people in living as independently as possible, and in ways they want to live. Still another goal is to support people with disabilities in having a normal life, and to live, work, and play with people who do not have disabilities.

Whenever one of the first three goals of positive behavior support is not reached because of problem behavior, then another goal of positive behavior support is to help overcome the problem. That is, we provide support to help individuals overcome problem behavior so they can:

- enjoy their lives

- live as independently as possible

- have a normal life

There are many tools in positive behavior support that help people with disabilities reach the just noted goals. We will describe and practice using these tools in our training sessions. However, positive behavior support is also based on important values. These values must be at the center of everything we do with positive behavior support.

## The Values of Positive Behavior Support

- **The first value of positive behavior support is respect for the rights of all citizens.**

The first value of positive behavior support is *respect for the rights of all citizens*. All staff should respect the human rights of all people supported by our agencies. We also want to remember that people with disabilities have the same rights as people without disabilities.

Most of you know what we are talking about -- rights that protect individuals from procedures that cause harm or hurt, rights that protect people from restraint without due process, the right to vote, and rights to privacy, just to name a few.

We will not go over each of the basic human rights here, because those are covered in other training that you have had. Our point here is that we must know these rights and support them. If you are not sure about the human rights that your agency supports, you should review them as soon as you can.

- **Another value of positive behavior support is the importance of the individual.**

Another value of positive behavior support is the *importance of the individual*. Positive behavior support must be person-centered. As many of you know, person-centered planning puts the person in control of which supports and services s/he receives as much as possible.

The values of person-centered planning and positive behavior support are the same. For example, an important part of both positive behavior support and person-centered planning is knowing that each person is an individual who has hopes and dreams. We must know what those hopes and dreams are, and support the hopes and dreams for each individual.

Like person-centered planning, positive behavior support cannot work unless we know each person very well. Before we can help a person overcome a problem behavior, we must get to know that individual. We must also take the time to find ways to interact with people in ways that they like. We will talk about ways to interact with people with disabilities in later classes.

Because positive behavior support values each person as an individual, we must know about the values that are important for each individual and each person's family. Many people come from different cultures, and we must take the time to learn what is important in their cultures and the cultures of their families.

- **A third value of positive behavior support is treating people with dignity.**

A third value of positive behavior support is *treating people with dignity.* Treating people with dignity means we treat people as people first, and we treat people in ways that they want to be treated.

Getting to know the people we support as people first means we do not think of them as having a particular label -- we think of

4

them as people who happen to have a type of disability. When we get to know individuals as people who have a disability instead of knowing them as *the disabled*, for example, then we are more likely to treat them with dignity just as we all want to be treated.

There are many ways we can promote dignity among individuals with disabilities. For example, we can talk to adults as adults and not as if we were talking to a child. We can also interact with people who have a disability during times that are normal to interact with anybody, such as during break times. We will talk more about how to promote dignity in later classes.

- **A final value of positive behavior support is that we must make sure people we support are not abused, neglected, or subjected to unnecessary restrictions.**

The human rights that we noted earlier talk about abuse and neglect, and describe what we must guard against. Making sure individuals are not abused and neglected is very important in positive behavior support.

Sometimes the people we support, like all of us, will need help in correcting things they do that can cause problems for them or other people. Correcting problem behavior is a part of positive behavior support and we will talk about ways to correct such behavior. However, we never correct behavior in a way that abuses or neglects an individual or restricts the person in ways that are not absolutely necessary.

Much of what we talk about with correcting behavior will be in the Behavior Support Plans (BSPs) of individuals. To make sure we provide correction in ways that respect people and do not abuse or neglect, we must always follow the way correction is written in the BSP or possibly a teaching plan. We will practice using BSPs in the right way in later classes.

As indicated earlier, positive behavior support has a number of tools. The different tools are used to support individuals in doing things that help them to enjoy their lives, and to live as independently and normally as possible.

## The ABC Model of Positive Behavior Support

Although the tools of positive behavior support are many, there is a basic way in which all the tools are used. This way is called the *ABC Model* of positive behavior support.

---

**ABC Model of Positive Behavior Support**

*A*ntecedent

*B*ehavior

*C*onsequence

---

At the center of the ABC model is *behavior* (the *B* part of the model). As just indicated, we support behavior that leads to the desired goals for the people we support.

We use many of our tools to make it likely that individuals will do things (i.e., their behavior) that will help them enjoy their lives and live independently and normally. We also use the tools to make it less likely that the people we support will have problem behavior.

We can use many tools of positive behavior support *before* individuals engage in certain behavior to make it likely that their behavior will benefit and not harm them or other people. Using tools before certain behavior occurs involves the *Antecedent* or *A* part of the ABC Model.

We also use tools *after* certain behaviors occur to make it more likely that future behavior will support an individual's goals, and less likely that problem behavior will occur. These tools involve the *consequences* for behavior. The consequences that occur as a result of a certain behavior make up the *C* part of the ABC Model.

In short, using the ABC Model in positive behavior support centers on:

- *Antecedents* -- events that take place before behavior occurs; for our purposes we look for antecedents that make it more likely desirable behavior will occur and problem behavior will not occur

- *Behavior* -- what an individual does

- *Consequences* -- events that take place after behavior occurs that make it more likely desirable behavior will occur in the future and problem behavior will not occur

We will describe in detail each of the parts of the ABC Model in the next sessions. We will then discuss in more detail how each of the parts can work together to support the goals and values we have discussed in this session.

# Module 2: Defining Behavior

## Objectives:

Upon completion of this module, trainees should be able to:

(1) Define behavior as anything a person does
(2) Identify behavior written in observable and measurable terms
(3) Describe behavior in observable, measurable terms so that others can agree when the behavior occurs

## What Is Behavior?

In the ABC model, "**B**" stands for behavior. A misunderstanding held by some people is that the word "behavior" means only something an individual does that is a problem. That is, aggression, self-injury, or tantrums, etc., are referred to as behaviors. The term behavior actually includes much more than just behavior problems.

Behavior is everything a person does. Behavior is the way in which people react or respond to their environment. Hitting another person is a behavior but so is crossing the street with the traffic light or typing on a keyboard.

Smiling, blinking, writing, talking, and even breathing are behaviors. To have no behavior, one would have to be dead!!

The main goal of positive behavior support in some ways is quite simple. Our goal is to develop strategies to increase behaviors that will help a person live a more independent and enjoyable life and to decrease behaviors that will interfere with a person's ability to live independently and enjoyably. Before we can learn how to provide positive behavior support, we must first learn to focus on a person's behavior.

# Defining Behavior

If positive behavior support is to develop ways to increase useful behavior and to decrease problem behavior, then those targeted behaviors must be clearly identified. If target behaviors are not clearly identified, staff will not know when or how to provide support for the person.   There are three rules we can follow to clearly identify target behaviors to be increased or decreased through positive behavior support.

---

### Defining a Target Behavior

Observable

Measurable

Others can agree

---

The first rule for identifying a target behavior is that the behavior must be described so that the behavior can be observed. Observable means that we can see when the behavior is occurring and not occurring. If it is a behavior it is someone's actions and we can *see* actions.

Suppose a target behavior to increase is understanding how to buy something from a vending machine. We will have difficulty implementing a plan of support for increasing this target behavior because "understanding" is not an observable behavior.

Although we cannot directly observe understanding or lack of understanding, we can describe the behaviors that show a person understands how to use a vending machine such as putting coins in the slot, pushing the selection, picking up the item, etc. These actions can be observed.

 Suppose a target behavior is to help a person feel more comfortable in his new neighborhood. Are we able to directly observe what a person feels? To use positive behavior support, we must describe the specific behaviors associated with how a person "feels", or what a person "understands".

Behavior should be described so that it is not only observable but can be measured. As will be discussed later in training, measurement is critical in helping us determine whether or not support plans are successful. We do not want to waste valuable time on procedures that do not work.

An example of an emotion that is not described in measurable terms is "anger". Anger cannot be measured very well unless we describe anger as a set of specific, observable behaviors. Observable behaviors can be measured.

Think of the behaviors a person does that let you know that person is angry. Can those behaviors be measured?

— hitting
— self injury
— Shouting
— Property damage

Finally, target behaviors must be defined clearly enough so that different people who provide support to an individual can agree when the behaviors occur.

 Suppose we identify "aggression" as a target behavior to decrease. Would everyone agree that pushing over a chair is aggression? Would everyone agree that a slight push of the chair is not aggression? If there is disagreement among staff as to when aggression is or is not occurring then the target behavior needs to be described more clearly.

Target behaviors must be defined clearly enough so that support providers can agree when a target behavior occurs so they know when and how to implement the Behavior Support Plan.

# Module 3: Positive Reinforcement and Punishment

## Objectives:                                          **Trainee Notes**

Upon completion of this module, trainees should be able to:

(1) Identify a positive reinforcing consequence by its effect on behavior
(2) Name at least two advantages of praise and feedback as reinforcers
(3) Demonstrate positive reinforcement to increase a target behavior
(4) Identify a punishing consequence by its effect on behavior

## Reinforcement and Punishment

In the ABC model, the "**C**" refers to the consequences that follow a behavior. Behavior can be increased or decreased based on the consequences that follow the behavior. We are going to talk about two types of consequences that have very different effects on behavior. These are *reinforcers* and *punishers*.

## Defining Positive Reinforcement

> **Positive Reinforcement**
>
> An individual *increases* behavior in order to get a desired consequence

The first type of consequence we will discuss is positive reinforcement. Positive reinforcers are consequences that follow a behavior and make it more likely the behavior will occur again in the future. In other words, when a person *increases* behavior in order to get a specific consequence, the consequence is acting as a positive reinforcer.

If you say hello to your co-workers when you see them in the morning and they return your greeting, you are likely to say hello to them on future mornings. When co-workers responded to your hello by greeting you in return, they *reinforced* your behavior. On the other hand, if you said hello to your co-workers each morning and they never returned your greeting, you are not as likely to continue saying hello to them each morning because your greeting behavior was not reinforced.

Sometimes we think of positive reinforcement as rewarding a person with something the person likes. However, positive reinforcement is more than a reward. *Positive reinforcement increases or improves behavior.*

The only way to know if a consequence is a positive reinforcer is to provide the consequence following a target behavior and see if the behavior *increases* over time. If the behavior does not increase, then the consequence is not acting as a positive reinforcer.

For example, I may enjoy coffee. However, if I was given a cup of coffee for completing a full day of work, it is not likely that I would work on future days to get another cup of coffee. Therefore, coffee is not a reinforcer for doing a day's work even though it is something I like.

**Sometimes positive reinforcers are a natural part of an activity.** For example when you make pizza, you get to eat the pizza.

| ? | Can you think of an example of a behavior, activity, or skill in which the reinforcer is a natural part of the activity for the people with whom you work? |

↳ taking meds → feeling better

*(handwritten, struck through)*

"Looking nice" should be the natural reinforcer for grooming tasks but looking nice may not be a reinforcer to some people at first.

| ? | Can you think of an example of a behavior, activity or skill in which the natural consequence does not act as a reinforcer? |

↳ Exersise → Sore muscles

When natural consequences of a behavior that we want to increase do not act as reinforcers, we must provide additional reinforcers to increase those behaviors. Therefore, we must identify items, events, or activities that will act as reinforcers.

## Everyone Has Individual Positive Reinforcers

**?** What are some items, events, or activities that reinforce your behavior? *Tea, Hot Chocolate, Stretching*

No single item or event is reinforcing to everyone. An important job of staff is to identify reinforcers that work for each individual.

---

### Identifying Possible Reinforcers

1. Ask the person. Also ask friends, family, or others who know the person well what the person likes

2. Observe to see how the person spends free time

3. Give a choice of items or activities to see what is chosen

4. Provide an item or activity after a behavior to see if the behavior increases over time

---

## Using Praise and Feedback as Reinforcers

The most common type of positive consequence used to increase behavior is praise and positive feedback. Praise and positive feedback are often reinforcers for people with and without disabilities. There are a number of advantages to using praise and feedback as positive reinforcers.

---

### Advantages of Using Praise and Feedback as Positive Reinforcers

Praise and feedback are always available and cost nothing to provide

It is typical for people with and without disabilities to receive praise and feedback

We rarely get tired of being praised

Praise and feedback can be provided without disrupting an ongoing activity

---

**?**   Would praise from someone you dislike positively reinforce your behavior? Why or why not?

Praise and feedback are not always positive reinforcers in all situations. Having a good relationship with a person helps make praise and feedback more likely to be positively reinforcing. Here are some ways that we can make our praise and feedback more reinforcing to the people whom we support.

---

### Keys to Building a Good Relationship

Spend time with an individual doing things the person likes to do

When possible, help the person to avoid things that are disliked

Learn to communicate well with each other

---

Having good relationships with the people around us adds to a good quality of life. All of us, including people with developmental disabilities, generally enjoy being around other people with whom we have a good relationship. We are less likely to enjoy people with whom we are unfamiliar or do not have a good relationship.

## Using **Reinforcement to Increase Behavior**

A reinforcer should be provided during or immediately following the behavior we want to increase. One reason we provide reinforcment immediately after a behavior we want to increase is that if we wait too long to provide the reinforcer, we may reinforce a behavior we had not planned to reinforce.

Reinforcement should never be provided following an undesirable behavior or any behavior we want to decrease.

## Defining Punishment

As we have just learned, positive reinforcement increases behavior because the person wants to get something liked. *Punishment* has the opposite effect on behavior.

---

**Punishment**

A person decreases a behavior because
the behavior is followed by an undesirable consequence

---

When a punisher follows a behavior, that behavior will decrease. A person does not want to experience the punisher so the person does not do the behavior that leads to punishment.

The term punishment is often misunderstood. It does not necessarily mean physical contact from the staff and it certainly does not mean abuse of any kind. Punishment is a natural result of some behaviors.

**?** Can you think of an example in which punishment is a natural result of a behavior or activity?

For example, if you eat too much spicy food, you may get sick. If you eat less spicy food in the future to avoid becoming sick, then getting sick was a punishing consequence for eating too much spicy food.

When an individual arrives late to work, the only jobs left to do are ones that are disliked. If late arrivals decrease, then the unpleasant work tasks are punishers for getting to work late.

Even when punishment is planned, punishment does not necessarily mean a very negative consequence.

Suppose every time I see you yawn in class, I call on you to answer a question. If you do not want to be called on to answer questions, you will try to stop yawning in class. Because I called on you when you yawned, yawning behavior was punished (if future yawning in class is decreased).

The only way we can tell a reinforcing consequence from a punishing consequence is by its effect on behavior.

For example, we might think that sending a person to a separate room when that person is disruptive is a negative consequence and therefore, a punisher for disruptive behavior. However, being alone is desired by some people and they will act out to obtain "alone" time. If so, sending the person to a separate room is likely to reinforce the disruptive behavior.

Again, the only way we can know if a consequence is a reinforcer or a punisher is to look at the effect the consequence has on future behavior. *Reinforcement increases the behavior it follows and punishment decreases the behavior it follows.*

# Module 4: Negative Reinforcement

**Objective:**                                          **Trainee Notes**

Upon completion of this module, trainees should be able to:

(1) Recognize examples of negative reinforcement in practical situations in settings with people who have developmental disabilities

## Positive Reinforcement

Earlier in class we talked about reinforcement and how it could be used to help support people with disabilities in many positive ways. To review briefly, reinforcement is the process of a behavior being followed by a consequence – that is, an item or event – that makes it more likely the behavior will occur again in the future. The consequence increases how often the person does the behavior.

---

**Positive Reinforcement**

A behavior is more likely to occur again because
the behavior allows a person to
get something that the person likes

---

To this point, we have talked about one type of reinforcement: *positive* reinforcement.

Positive reinforcement increases a behavior because the resulting consequence of the behavior is something positive for the person; the person will work to get the consequence. For example, praise from a support staff following a person's desired behavior can reinforce that behavior because many people with developmental disabilities, like us, will work to be praised.

# Negative Reinforcement

In this class session we will be talking about another type of reinforcement: *negative* reinforcement. Just like positive reinforcement, negative reinforcement involves a consequence following a behavior that makes it more likely the behavior will occur again in the future. However, *the type of consequence involved in negative reinforcement is quite different than that involved in positive reinforcement.*

---

**Negative Reinforcement**

A behavior is more likely to occur again because the behavior allows a person to stop something that the person dislikes or finds unpleasant

---

When thinking about negative reinforcement, it is important for us to know that the process is not something that is actually negative for a person. Instead, the process makes a situation more desirable for a person by *removing* something that the person does not like (something negative for the individual is stopped or taken away).

***When something a person does not like is removed after a certain behavior, the person is more likely to do the behavior again.*** Because the behavior allows the individual to stop or remove something that is unwanted, the behavior is reinforced. Again, just like positive reinforcement, negative reinforcement always increases how often a behavior occurs.

To show how negative reinforcement works, think about sitting in your yard and a bug lands on your face. You slap at the bug with your hand and the bug goes away. In this case, your slapping behavior was most likely *negatively reinforced* because it caused the (unwanted) bug to go away. So the next time a bug lands on you what are you likely to do? (Answer: Slap it!).

As another example, think about when a person we support does not want to do a required activity such as having her teeth brushed by a support staff. The person with a disability may strike out at the staff or push the toothbrush away. The support staff then stops the teeth brushing. This is how the consequence or activity of the support person stopping the teeth brushing will *negatively reinforce* the individual's aggressive behavior.

Because the aggressive behavior of the person with a disability stopped the brushing, the person is more likely to act out in the future during teeth brushing because the aggression will stop the teeth brushing.

It can be helpful to think about negative reinforcement using the ABC Model of positive behavior support that we have talked about.

In the example just given, the individual behavior of concern is aggression or hitting. The antecedent is the staff person starting the teeth brushing, and the consequence – in this case a consequence resulting in negative reinforcement – is stopping of the teeth brushing.

As we will talk about later, one way to prevent the aggression from occurring would be to make the teeth brushing activity more enjoyable for the individual, so the person would have no reason to try (i.e., with aggression) to have the activity stopped.

 Think about your own work situation. Can you think of examples in which a person you support has used problem behavior to stop an activity the person did not like, or to have something removed that the person found unpleasant?

## Using Positive versus Negative Reinforcement

Negative reinforcement occurs often in the lives of people with and without disabilities. It is important to note that this is a type of *reinforcement* and it increase how often a behavior occurs. However, because negative reinforcement involves *removing* things a person does not like – that is, a person behaves in order to stop something that is unwanted – this is not always a pleasant means of helping people change behavior.

Our focus is on *positive* behavior support. In our interactions with people we support, we should always try to use positive reinforcement.

*Although we should use positive reinforcement as much as possible, we should be aware of when negative reinforcement happens with people we support.*

We should be very aware of when an individual uses problem behavior to stop or get rid of something the person does not like. In these cases we must try to change the situations so that there is no need for the problem behavior.

Other sessions will describe ways to change these types of situations by making activities more pleasant and positive for people we support (for example, by providing choice of activities; making activities more *positively* reinforcing). Other sessions will also talk about how to teach people with disabilities useful ways to communicate the need to change things they do not like without using problem behavior.

# Module 5: Identification of Antecedents, Behaviors, and Consequences

**Objectives:**                                  **Trainee Notes**

Upon completion of this module, trainees should be able to:

(1) Describe how the parts of the Antecedent, Behavior, Consequence (ABC) model work together in positive behavior support
(2) Identify parts of the ABC model when presented with life-like scenarios

## Review of Behavior and Consequences

To this point we have talked about *behavior* and *consequences* in positive behavior support. We have described how positive and negative reinforcing consequences increase how often a behavior occurs. We have also discussed how punishing consequences decrease how often a behavior occurs.

## Antecedents

| **Definition of an Antecedent** |
| --- |
| An antecedent is an event that occurs before a behavior and makes it more likely that the behavior will occur |

Behavior and consequences make up part of the ABC Model. In this class we will talk in more detail about antecedents. To review, ***an antecedent is an event that occurs before a behavior.*** In positive behavior support we are most interested in those antecedents ***that occur before a behavior and make it more likely the behavior will occur.***

---

**Examples of Typical Antecedents to Behavior**

1. Suad's dad *places a magazine on a table in front of her* and Suad immediately begins the leisure activity of looking at the magazine.

2. Tyrone *sits down next to Samuel on the sofa* and Samuel begins to hit his forehead with his palm.

3. Rasheed *sits down next to Samuel on the sofa* and Samuel smiles broadly.

4. Mary *begins hopping and whining* and then knocks over a chair.

---

## The ABC Model

When we use positive behavior support to help individuals with developmental disabilities lead enjoyable, independent, and normal lives without problem behavior, we must think about each of the three parts of the ABC Model.

---

**ABC Model**

$A$ntecedent

$B$ehavior

$C$onsequence

---

- **antecedents** - events that occur before a behavior

- **behavior** - what a person does

- **consequences** - items or events that follow the behavior

When the three parts of the ABC Model are used together, we have a very good way to understand and reduce problem behavior. We also have a very good way to understand and increase desirable behavior. Specifically, we can use the ABC Model to:

- Teach a useful skill

- Increase desired behavior

- Decrease problem behavior

- Understand why certain behaviors occur

In order to use the ABC model to support people and to prevent or change problem behavior, it is important to know how the model works in everyday situations for individuals with whom we work.

There are many ways to use the ABC model as part of positive behavior support. We will be discussing and practicing these ways in later class sessions. For our purposes at this point, it is important to be able to identify each part of the model in action.

It is also important to know a basic rule for using the ABC model to help people with disabilities increase desirable behavior and decrease or prevent problem behavior.

---

**Basic Rule for Using the ABC Model**

Provide antecedents and positive reinforcing consequences for desirable behavior and where possible, remove or change antecedents that come before problem behavior

---

We provide antecedents and positive reinforcing consequences for desirable behavior. Also, we try to remove or change antecedents that lead to problem behavior. In other words, *we can use the ABC model to help people do those things that help them live independently and enjoyably, and to help prevent problem behavior.* Again, we will be discussing how to use the ABC model for these purposes in many of the remaining class sessions.

# Module 6: Setting Events

**Objectives**                                                **Trainee Notes**

Upon completion of this module, trainees should be able to:

(1) Define a setting event as something that at a later time
    changes how an antecedent or consequence affects a
    person's behavior
(2) Identify setting events that change how antecedents affect
    a person's behavior
(3) Identify setting events that change how consequences
    affect a person's behavior

## Introducing Setting Events

We have discussed how antecedents and consequences affect
behavior. There are also events that can change how certain
antecedents and consequences affect an individual's behavior.
The most important of these are *setting events*.

Setting events are experiences a person has that, at a later time,
cause a certain antecedent or consequence to affect the person's
behavior differently than it usually does. Setting events *set the
occasion* for certain behavior to occur or not occur later by
causing an antecedent or consequence to have a different effect
on a person's behavior. Setting events may happen an hour or so
before the actual behavior or even several days before the
behavior.

31

You may know a person you support who acts differently when he returns to his group home after spending a holiday with relatives at their home. He may act out more than usual to get attention from staff. Something happened at the relatives' home or upon leaving home – a setting event – that makes attention more desired than usual when he returns. Perhaps he misses his relatives and feels lonely. As a result, he wants more attention than usual from staff and has learned to act out more to get it.

Another individual may receive a new medication one morning that reduces her appetite. Later that day at lunch she does not eat her meal. Receiving the new medication was a setting event that later caused the lunch meal to be less desired than usual. That is why she did not eat her lunch.

> **?**    Can you think of examples of events that affect how a person you support behaves differently at a later point in time?

When thinking about examples of setting events, it is important to see how the events changed how an antecedent or consequence affected an individual's behavior differently than it usually does. Remember, setting events change how an antecedent or consequence affects behavior.

Identifying how an event changes the typical effect of an antecedent or consequence on some future behavior can be difficult. This often takes detailed assessment by someone with behavioral expertise. Generally, when you think that a person's behavior is being affected by something that happened in the past, you should seek help from your behavioral professional.

However, it is still important to have a general understanding of setting events. That is our purpose here – to provide a general understanding of setting events and how they affect future behavior. Let's look at an example of how an event that occurs at one time changes how an antecedent affects behavior at a later time.

---

**Example of A Setting Event Changing How An Antecedent Affects Behavior**

Your supervisor had a bad start to her day. She had an unpleasant argument with her husband before coming to work that put her in a "bad mood" (*setting event*). When you asked her for some help with something at work (*antecedent*) she responded curtly by saying "Not now; can't you see I have my own work to do!" (her *behavior*). Such behavior is very unlike how she usually responds to your request, which is typically pleasant and helpful.

---

In this case, the unpleasant argument (resulting in a "bad mood") could be a setting event for a "problem behavior" involving the supervisor's unpleasant response. The argument changed how the antecedent (your request for help) affected the supervisor's behavior that usually followed that antecedent. Instead of responding to your request with helpful advice, the supervisor responded in a negative, nonhelpful manner.

Now let's look at an example of how a setting event may change the role of a consequence on a person's behavior.

---

**Example of A Setting Event Changing How A Consequence Affects Behavior**

A person with a disability does not like the breakfast served in her group home and does not eat it (*setting event*). Later at her supported job she repeatedly leaves her work table to go get her lunch box (her *behavior*) and something to eat (*consequence*). This is not her usual work behavior as she typically works very hard. Her job coach (who does not know about her not eating breakfast) is concerned that she keeps leaving her work and does not complete it. Because this pattern of repeatedly leaving her work to get something to eat has happened on other days, the job coach reports she needs a Behavior Support Plan (BSP) to keep her from leaving her work table during the morning.

---

Here, the setting event is not eating breakfast, such that the person is hungry during the morning at work. On the days she does not eat breakfast, food is a much more powerful consequence for getting something to eat than on days she eats breakfast. Hence, on the days she does not eat breakfast she is more likely to leave her work table (to get something to eat).

To help the person stay at her table and work, the setting event should be addressed. That is, the person should have a breakfast she likes and eats every morning. Trying to reduce her leaving the work table with a BSP that targets only that behavior without changing the setting event would not be addressing the true problem. It would also likely make being at the table unpleasant for the individual because she is still hungry.

We must make sure that when we think something is working as a setting event, we can tell how the event likely changes the role of an antecedent or consequence for a certain behavior. If we cannot determine this, we probably have not identified a true setting event. Also, we would likely be trying to explain why an individual does something based on a previous event that really has no effect on the later behavior of concern. Again, identifying setting events usually requires assessment by a behavioral professional.

# Module 7: Meaningful and Integrated Day Supports

**Objectives:**                **Trainee Notes**

Upon completion of this module, trainees should be able to:

(1) Describe how day supports vary from meaningful to nonmeaningful
(2) Identify examples of day supports that are and are not integrated in the community
(3) Describe how to change from a segregated day activity to a community-integrated activity

## Meaningful and Integrated Day Supports

A key part of positive behavior support is making sure people with disabilities have meaningful and integrated activities to engage in which include day supports. In this session we will provide an overview of what this means. Later sessions provide more specific information, such as how to make sure the skills we teach to individuals are truly meaningful and functional.

## Meaningful Day Supports

First, let's look at what meaningful supports mean. We will talk mainly about day supports provided during routine weekdays. We will also talk some about weekends and other leisure times.

---

**Continuum of Meaningful Day Supports**

**Usually Most Meaningful**

Working in a real job in the community for real pay, either independently or with support

Supported work on a work crew or enclave in the community

Sheltered, contract work in an agency or center

Nonwork activities in an agency or center

**Usually Least Meaningful**

---

The above continuum shows what the professional field in developmental disabilities considers day supports that are more meaningful versus less meaningful. It is also important to know that current funding and standards for adult services go along with this continuum. For example, the Medicaid Waiver Program is increasingly funding only those services that provide the most meaningful and integrated day supports.

The most meaningful day supports occur when an adult with an intellectual or other developmental disability is involved in a real job for real pay.

**?**      Why do you think it is important for people with disabilities to have real jobs for real pay?

Working in real jobs for real pay allows people to earn an income, and receive the dignity and increased independence that one receives by being part of the country's workforce. It also means people with disabilities are integrated within a main part of society – they work alongside people without disabilities.

Supporting people to get and keep real jobs is the first goal of positive behavior support for providing meaningful day supports. Of course, many people have challenges that make it difficult to work totally by themselves. However, these individuals often can have supported jobs in which they receive help from paid staff such as individual job placements with the help of job coaches. It is also becoming more common for a person with a disability to receive assistance from co-workers.

Supported jobs also include crews or enclaves, in which people with disabilities work together in the community to perform a job.

 Can you think of examples of work crews or enclaves that you have seen or worked with?

Work crews and enclaves are generally viewed as the second most meaningful day supports. They involve real, paid work in the community. However, because the workers with disabilities work primarily with each other instead of other people, this type of work is not as integrated within society as individual job placements.

You most likely know what contract work is. People work with supervision in an agency or center such as a sheltered workshop making a product. The agency has a contract with a company that pays for the product. People with disabilities are usually paid based on the amount of work products they complete.

 What do you think are some of the pros and cons of contract work?

Contract work allows people with disabilities to earn an income, although it is usually much less than with jobs in the community. Sometimes contract work is provided with the intent to help individuals learn work skills that will lead to typical jobs. However, history has shown that most people who work in agencies doing contract work never "graduate" to typical jobs in the community. Contract work in agencies also involves little if any community integration. In this situation extra effort is needed to support their meaningful community integration.

The biggest concerns with the meaningfulness of day supports is often when people with disabilities are in an agency doing nonwork activities. It can be very difficult for staff to support individuals in meaningful activity participation when they are in a large room or classroom and there is no paid work for them to do.

 Can you think of some nonwork activities you have seen in which people with disabilities have been involved in an agency that did not seem meaningful?

Some common activities that occur in this situation involve adults putting child puzzles together day after day, looking at the same magazine over and over, or just sitting with nothing else to do. These types of activities do not meet the goals of positive behavior support to help people with developmental disabilities learn to live as independently and enjoyably as possible. We will talk more about meaningful versus nonmeaningful activities that do not involve paid work in agencies or centers later.

## Integrated Day Supports

The way that day supports help people with disabilities be integrated within society generally goes along with the continuum of meaningful day supports. That is, real jobs involve the most integration, work crews and enclaves less integration but more than contract work in agencies, and nonwork activities in agencies have about the same or less integration than contract work.

A key goal of positive behavior support is to promote integration of the people we support within every day society. As we just talked about, helping people get and keep real jobs is one way to help them be integrated in society. We should also promote integration during other daily activities when individuals are not working.

There are different ways to help people with developmental disabilities be involved in integrated, community activities beyond work. Below are two of the most common ways.

---

**Examples of Two Common Types of
Community Activities**

1. The same types of community *leisure and recreational activities* in which we and other people participate.

2. *Volunteering* in community agencies and services.

---

One way is to support individual involvement in the same types of community leisure and recreational activities in which we and other people participate. These can include spectator events such as going to watch athletic events and to movie theaters. They can also involve activities that include more active participation, such as eating in restaurants, shopping, using the gym, or going fishing.

To actively participate in community events, people must have the skills to participate. This is another reason later sessions focus on selecting meaningful or functional skills to teach to individuals, and how to teach these important skills.

Another common way to support community integration is through volunteer activities. This may involve supporting individuals in volunteering to help at food shelters, animal care facilities, recycling centers, and plant nurseries.

 Can you think of examples of other types of volunteer activities you have experienced with people who have developmental disabilities?

During this class some of you may have been thinking that many people you work with have such serious challenges that it would be very hard to regularly promote their active involvement in community activities. It can be very hard, and require re-evaluation of how we use our resources or even getting more resources.

Still, this is what we must work toward. This is also where person-centered planning can help. When done right, person-centered planning typically includes community members who may be able to help with certain efforts without extra cost.

Funding sources for many agencies are demanding more community integration. Soon they will likely fund only agency supports and services that are truly integrated in the community. More importantly, we should strive for community integration because it provides many benefits for people with developmental disabilities.

When people with developmental disabilities participate in the same types of community settings and activities that we do, they have more opportunities to:

- Interact with and learn from other people

- Develop new skills, interests, and preferences that allow for more daily enjoyment

- Be viewed by people in general with more dignity and be accepted as an important part of society just like everybody else

- Develop friendships with people in their communities

# Module 8: Teaching Functional Skills

**Objectives:**                                              **Trainee Notes**

Upon completion of this module, trainees should be able to:

(1) Describe guidelines for selecting functional (meaningful) skills to teach
(2) Identify examples of functional and nonfunctional skills

## What Skills Should We Teach?

In previous modules, we discussed that a goal of positive behavior support is to increase behaviors that help a person live an independent, integrated, enjoyable life and to decrease behaviors that reduce independence and enjoyment. We also talked about the importance of meaningful day supports for achieving this goal.

We also talked about important teaching tools for increasing behavior such as antecedents and positive reinforcement. Later, we will talk about other ways to teach new behaviors. Before we learn more about *how* to teach though, we should spend some time discussing *what* to teach. We want to make sure what we teach is truly meaningful or *functional* for each individual.

45

# Guidelines for Deciding What to Teach

Some skills are more useful than others in helping people live independent, enjoyable lives. Skills that help people to function in the places they live, work, and play are *functional skills*.

When deciding what skills are important to teach, several guidelines can help us be sure we are choosing functional skills. However, along with the guidelines, the strengths, needs, current living situation, and future dreams of people with developmental disabilities should be considered when deciding the most useful skills to teach.

---

### Guideline #1

*A functional skill is an activity that someone else would have to do for the person if the person could not to do the activity*

---

Typically, the more control we have over how we live, the more we enjoy our lives. A key to controlling how we live is being able to do as many of the activities needed for daily living as possible without having to depend on others for support. One way to look at the usefulness of a skill is whether or not someone would have to perform the skill for us if we could not do it for ourselves.

If we do not know how to put on a coat, this action would have to be done by someone else for us because we usually do not want to go out in the cold without a coat. Therefore, putting on a coat is a functional skill to teach.

46

Shopping for food at the grocery store is a functional skill because someone would have to buy food for us if we could not buy our own food.

In contrast, pointing to pictures of coats in a magazine is not something that someone would have to do for us if we could not do it ourselves. Pointing to pictures in magazines probably does little to help a person live an independent and enjoyable life; it is not a functional skill.

Sorting plastic (toy) food items into basic food groups also would not be a functional teaching activity because no one would have to sort toy food items by food groups for us if we could not do it ourselves.

---

### Guideline #2

*The more often a skill is needed, the more useful the skill is to teach.*

---

If we were to follow a person we support during the day and list all activities that staff had to do for the individual, we would probably have a long list of functional skills that we could teach to the person. However, some of the activities on the list may involve skills that are needed a lot more often than others. The more often a skill is needed, the more useful the skill is to learn.

Greeting other people by saying or signing "Hello" is a useful skill to teach because it is likely to be needed several times a day.

Staff may have to help a person use a taxi. However, if using a taxi is a skill that is needed only a few times a year or less, it is less useful than skills a person needs on a daily or even weekly basis.

 Can you think of a skill that is functional because it is often needed and a skill that is not as functional because it is not often needed?

---

**Guideline 3**

*Skills for taking part in age-apppropriate activities are generally more functional than skills for taking part in age-inappropriate activities*

---

Individuals with developmental disabilities are more likely to be accepted in typical communities if they behave like their peers without disabilities. In this manner, doing the kinds of activities expected of someone of the same age promotes dignity among people with developmental disabilities. It can also promote inclusion in the typically occurring activities in community settings.

When people with disabilities can do the kinds of activities that their peers without disabilities do and enjoy, they have more chances to do things with other people.

For example, if people with disabilities have the skills to participate in age-appropriate leisure activities, they can use the same community resources that people without disabilities depend on for leisure such as the swimming pool, park, mall, etc.

Teaching an adult to feed the ducks at a park is more functional than teaching an adult to play with toy trucks. People in typical communities are likely to shy away from adults who play with toy trucks in the park!

Teaching a teenager to dance to rock music would be more functional than teaching a teenager to do the "Hokey Poky." A teenager who can dance to rock music will be more accepted at a school dance than one who only does the Hokey Poky.

---

### Guideline #4

*Skills that allow a person to get something
wanted or get out of something unwanted
without problem behavior are functional.*

---

Earlier we talked about how some behavior problems develop as a way for a person to get something that is wanted (the behavior problem is positively reinforced) or to get out of something that is not wanted (the behavior problem is negatively reinforced).

One way to reduce problem behavior is to teach more appropriate ways to get something wanted or out of something that is unwanted. An appropriate skill that *replaces* problem behavior as a way of getting something wanted or getting out of something unwanted is a functional skill. It is also a useful communication skill.

A person may learn that a way to leave the dining room quickly after mealtime is to throw a plate. It would be useful to teach an acceptable way for letting staff know the person wants to leave the dining room. Putting the napkin on the plate or carrying dishes to the sink may be acceptable behaviors for replacing plate throwing.

# The Teaching Setting and Materials Are Important

The teaching setting and materials can affect the usefulness of the skills we teach. Ideally, we should teach in the same setting where the skill is needed. Also, the teaching materials should be the same materials the person would normally use to complete the skill. People with developmental disabilities and in particular severe disabilities, have difficulty applying skills learned in one situation to other situations.

If it is not possible to teach in the setting where the skill is needed and to use actual materials, then the more similar we can make the teaching setting and materials to "real life," the more likely we are to be teaching functional skills.

---

**The Teaching Setting and Materials**

Teach in the setting where the skill is needed
using materials the person would normally use
or
Make the teaching setting and materials as similar as possible
to "real life" settings and materials

---

We are more likely to teach functional time-telling skills if we use real clocks or a cell phone as teaching materials instead of flash cards printed with clock faces or plastic toy clocks with movable arms.

Useful money skills are not likely to be taught using activities like counting play money or matching pictures of coins. Useful money skills are likely to be taught at stores, restaurants, etc., using real money as teaching materials. That is, skills *should be taught in the same manner or context in which the skills would be used.*

# Review of the Importance of Teaching Functional Skills

One of the values on which positive behavior support is based is the importance of treating people with dignity. When people with disabilities can do useful things, they are likely to be treated with more respect by others. Independence results in feelings of pride and self-worth, and promotes dignity and inclusion in their community.

51

---

**Review of The Importance of Teaching Functional Skills**

Promotes Dignity

Helps People Learn Skills More Quickly and
Apply Skills to New Situations

Prevents Problem Behavior

---

A goal of positive behavior support is to help people with disabilities live as independently as possible. Individuals can be more independent if we teach skills that are often needed and useful in different settings. As individuals practice new skills in different settings, it becomes easier for them to apply the skills learned in one setting to other new settings.

A final reason why teaching functional skills is important to positive behavior support relates to preventing problem behavior. When people engage in meaningless, unenjoyable activities, problem behavior is more likely to occur. On the other hand, when people have learned functional skills that allow them to use their time doing enjoyable, useful things, problem behavior is less likely.

# Module 9: Role of the Environment

**Objectives:**                                                    **Trainee Notes**

Upon completion of this module, trainees should be able to:

(1) Identify the effects of environments on a person's enjoyment, independence, and problem behavior
(2) Identify four desired characteristics of environments for positive behavior support

## Importance of the Environment

The quality of a person's life depends in large part on the person's environment. The environment means the type of place where a person lives, works, and plays. The environment also means whom a person interacts with on a day-to-day basis, as well as the quality of those interactions.

| How the Environment Affects Positive Behavior Support |
|---|
| 1. The environment affects a person's daily enjoyment |
| 2. The environment affects learning and using important life skills |
| 3. The environment affects whether problem behavior will occur |

The environment of people with developmental disabilities plays an important part in positive behavior support. The environment affects quality of life and positive behavior support in many ways. However, there are three most important ways.

- The most important way an environment affects positive behavior support is an individual's enjoyment with day-to-day activities. We want environments chosen by people with disabilities that help them to do activities that they enjoy, to do things with materials that they like, and to have many positive interactions with a variety of different people.

- The second way environments affect positive behavior support is that when environments help people with disabilities do things they like to do, then they learn useful skills and have many chances to use those skills – hopefully in typical, integrated settings. Doing useful things also gives people with developmental disabilities chances to receive a lot of positive reinforcement from support staff and others.

- The third way environments affect positive behavior support stems from the first two ways. That is, when people enjoy their environment and are active in useful and meaningful ways, problem behavior is not likely to occur.

Because of the importance of the environment on life enjoyment and positive behavior support, we must make sure we provide the right kinds of environments for people with disabilities. There are many important things to look for in a person's environment. However, there are four most important things.

---

**Important Things to Look For in an Environment**

    1. Choices

    2. If it is a typical environment

    3. Suited to individual needs

    4. Preferred items and events

---

The first thing to look for in an environment is whether people with disabilities have many *choices*. When individuals make many choices during the day (e.g., choice of what activity to do, choice of whom to interact with), they are more likely to enjoy themselves and be actively engaged in meaningful activities.

One of the most important choices for people with disabilities is the environment in which the person lives, works, and plays. As much as possible, people we support should choose the environments in which they spend their time. It is also worth noting that whether a person chooses where to live and whom to live with is one area on which community support agencies are evaluated.

Again, when people make many and important choices, they enjoy their lives more than if someone else makes choices for them. Daily enjoyment means problem behavior is not likely to happen. We will talk more about how to provide choices in later class sessions.

The second thing to look for in an environment is how *typical* the environment appears. By typical, we mean that the environment is like the environments in which people without disabilities live, work, and play.

Having a typical environment also means an individual spends a lot of time in regular communities. Regular communities are where most people who do not have disabilities spend their time.

Typical environments support individuals with disabilities in learning and using skills that are useful and meaningful to them. As we talked about earlier, when a person has and practices useful skills, problem behavior is not likely to happen and outcomes meaningful to the person are likely to result.

A third important thing to look for in an environment is how well the environment suits individual wants and needs. Environments must be suitable for each person in the environment. For example, the way the environment is set up should be suitable to the person's age; adults should not have to live or play in environments that are set up for children.

The environment must also suit each person's physical disabilities (if a person has a physical disability). Environments must be set up for wheelchairs in some cases, with easy ways to go outside or inside, and for people with disabilities to get to the things they want.

The fourth thing to look for in an environment is preferred items and events of people with disabilities. We must know what each person likes, and make sure those things are present in the environment every day.

When each of the things just noted is in place in the environments of people we support, then problem behavior is not likely to happen. If problem behavior does occur however, it is important to look at the environment in which the behavior occurs to see if these types of things are in place. If they are not in place, we must change the environment.

Looking at the environment and making changes where needed should occur before a Behavior Support Plan (BSP) is talked about for an individual's problem behavior.

---

**First step of positive behavior support plans:**
look at the good things in a person's environment

---

That is, the first step when thinking about a BSP for an individual's problem behavior is to look at, and where necessary improve, the environment. One way to look at an environment is to think about the good and bad things in the environment *from the person's perspective.*

When there are more bad things in someone's environment, our job is to change the environment to make more good things happen for the person.

---

**_Problem_ behavior
cannot be treated in a _problem_ environment**

---

In short, one cannot treat problem behavior if the behavior occurs in a problem environment. If the things we have talked about are not present in the every day environment, then that environment is most likely a problem. In later class sessions we will be talking more about how to change environments to make them as pleasant as possible for people we support.

# Module 10: The Role of Choice

**Objectives:**                                              **Trainee Notes**

Upon completion of this module, trainees should be able to:

(1) Identify the importance of choice for enjoying life
(2) Demonstrate how to provide a choice to individuals
   who do not talk
(3) Identify when to give choices
(4) Identify positive outcomes of giving choices

## The Importance of Choice in Our Lives

Having choice means having control over our lives. Typically, the more control we have over our lives, the more enjoyable our lives become. Choice is important to people with disabilities in the same way that choice is important to us. Choice is an important part of both positive behavior support and person-centered supports and services.

We typically make more choices than can be counted each day, but research has shown that people with developmental disabilities usually make few choices.

| ? | Why do you think people with disabilities have few choice opportunities? |
|---|---|

There are probably many reasons why people with developmental disabilities have few choice opportunities.

- We may be concerned that bad choices will be harmful

- Some agencies, and mainly agencies serving groups of people, do not have the resources for individual choices

- We do not know how to offer choices to people who do not understand what we say and who are unable to talk

The first two reasons for few choices must be addressed on a person-by-person basis within an agency. However, a third reason – not knowing how to offer choices to people who are unable to talk – is a problem we will discuss during this training.

## Different Ways of Making Choices

| *Difficulty of Choice Making* | | | | |
|---|---|---|---|---|
| **Easy**<br>**(requires less skills)** | | | | **Hard**<br>**(requires more skills)** |
| 1-item choice | 2-item choice with objects | 2-item choice with pictures | Vocal choice (naming items) | Vocal choice (open-ended) |

Some different ways people can make choices are listed above. Note that whether the choice making is easy or hard pertains to the individual making the choice. Hard choices require more skills for an individual and easy choices require less skills. The way we should present a choice depends on the choice-making skills of each person. Some people can tell us what they do and do not want. For these people, we simply ask them what they want and they tell us either by talking, signing, or using a communication aid.

---

**Steps for Giving a Vocal Choice**

- Ask individual what s/he would like (What would you like to do?, What would you like to eat?, What color of paint would you like to use?, etc.)

- If individual does not respond with a choice or if the choice named is not available, name two available alternatives for choice (Would you like to watch TV or listen to the stereo?, Would you like a Coke or a Sprite?, etc.)

- When the individual responds by naming an available option, provide the named option

---

For people who have a hard time understanding what we say and telling us what they want, we must present choices so that they can make a choice in an easier way. As we move from right to left along the line, choice making becomes easier in terms of requiring less skills.

Some people can make choices when shown pictures or symbols that represent choices. Others can make choices only when given actual objects from which to choose. At the far left of the line is the most simple form of choice making. People with multiple, severe disabilities sometimes need to have objects given one at a time to make a choice.

We will practice providing choices for people with the most significant disabilities who do not talk, sign, or use communication aids because providing choices for these individuals is often most difficult for support staff.

---

**Steps for Giving a 2-Item Choice Using Objects**

- Show the person two items and ask the person to choose one item

- If the person does not pick an item, let the person sample both items (a few seconds to interact with each material or taste food items)

- After the person samples both items, present both items again

- Ask the person to pick one of the items

- After the person picks an item, remove the second item and give the person the chosen item

---

As noted before, the simplest form of giving a choice is presenting a single item. When a single item is presented, staff should watch the person to see if he/she approaches or avoids the item.

An approach might include smiling, reaching for, leaning toward, or looking at the item. When a person approaches an item, the person should receive the item.

Avoidance might include turning away from the item, pushing the item away, or frowning. When a person avoids a presented item, the item should be removed.

Many times a person may not approach or avoid an item. Lack of approach and avoidance is called neutral behavior. When neutral behavior is shown, we should allow the person to sample the item, then give the item again to check for approach or avoidance. If neutral behavior occurs the second time an item is given, the item should be removed.

---

### Steps for Giving a 1-Item Choice

1. Present one item where the person can see it

2. Observe for approach, avoidance, or neutral behavior

3.   A. If approach occurs, provide the item

    B. If avoidance occurs, remove the item

    C. If neutral behavior occurs, let the person sample the item

4. After the person gets to know the item, present the item again

5. Observe for approach, avoidance, or neutral behavior

6. If approach occurs, provide item; if avoidance or neutral behavior occurs, remove the item

---

# Identifying When to Give Choices
# During the Day

| Types of Choices |
| --- |

What?                    How?                    When?

            Where?                    With whom?

Sometimes choices involve what to do. In other words, these are choices between activities (e.g., get out of bed or sleep later). Other choices involve how to do an activity (e.g., bathe by taking a shower or taking a bath). Still other types of choices involve when to do an activity, where to do an activity, and with whom to do the activity.

By making different types of choices part of the daily routine, such routines can be more enjoyable for the people we support. Think about the routines of the people you support when you return to work. Then think about the different types of choices and how you could build more choices into their routines.

In this class we have focused our discussion of choice making mainly on people who have difficulty communicating their choices. However, we must remember that giving and honoring choices are just as important for people who communicate well. All individuals can benefit from having the chance to make many choices.

# Beneficial Effects of Choice

---

Identifies individual likes

Increases enjoyment of life

Identifies potential reinforcers

Increases work and leisure activities

Reduces behavior problems

---

Giving frequent choices can result in a number of nice outcomes for individuals. One outcome is that repeated choice-making by a person gives staff an idea of what that person likes.

Giving people choices increases their daily enjoyment; when they make a choice they are by definition choosing something they prefer or enjoy (relative to what they do not choose). Also, if we give a person many opportunities to choose, for example, what to have for breakfast each morning, we may begin to see that some foods are chosen more than others. If we know what a person likes, then when a choice cannot be given, we know what items or activities to provide that the person is likely to enjoy.

Knowing what people like is a big part of positive behavior support. As noted earlier, knowing what someone likes can help identify reinforcers. Items and activities that people choose are more likely to act as reinforcers than items and activities that staff choose for individuals.

Research has shown that people are more likely to take part in activities they choose or enjoy than activities that they do not enjoy or that have been chosen for them. When people are doing things they enjoy doing, they are less likely to have problem behavior.

# Module 11: Interactions

**Objectives:**

Upon completion of this module, trainees should be able to:

(1) Demonstrate how to provide frequent, positive interactions for all individuals in a group
(2) Demonstrate how to observe and evaluate interactions in a group
(3) Demonstrate how to use social interactions to diffuse a situation likely to result in a problem behavior

## Importance of Social Interactions

Earlier in class we discussed the importance of social interactions on quality of life. To review briefly, interacting frequently with the people we support helps us to get to know them well. Frequent interactions are also an important part of positive behavior support, help prevent or reduce problem behavior, and can increase the quality of life for the people with disabilities whom we support.

## Characteristics of Supportive Interactions

In addition to the importance of social interactions on quality of life, *how* interactions are provided for people we support is important. There are three general guidelines for interactions that typically are useful to follow in most service settings for people with developmental disabilities.

To help prevent problem behavior, interacting in the way shown with the guidelines serves as an antecedent for desirable behavior among people with disabilities whom we support. That is, interactions can make it more likely desirable behavior will occur, and less likely that problem behavior will occur.

---

**Guidelines for Interacting with People We Support**

Interact with all people
Interact in a positive way
Interact in an appropriate way...
Use person's way
For the person's age

---

In many situations you are responsible for a group of individuals (for example, in a group home, on a work crew, or in a classroom). When working with groups, it is important to interact with every person present.

In order to interact with all individuals in a group, it is usually necessary to limit the interactions to a minute or less with each person in order to have time to rotate interactions frequently across all people present. Of course, how often one interacts with each individual in the group should depend on the nature of each individual's needs and ongoing activity.

For example, for individuals at work on a job, interactions should not occur so often that the interactions interrupt work. But in an informal leisure situation during the evening in a group home, it would generally be desirable to have brief, frequent interactions with each individual. These could be, for example, positive comments about a person's work efforts or a simple greeting.

Longer interactions with one individual at a time can occur when there are several staff present so that while one staff interacts continuously with one person, other staff can have brief interactions with the other individuals.

A second guideline for interacting with a group of individuals with developmental disabilities is to be *positive.* Positive interactions that show some type of approval or simply involve saying something nice are the types of interactions we all tend to like. Negative interactions that include some type of disapproval represent the types of interactions we tend to dislike.

| Positive Interactions | Negative Interactions |
|---|---|
| Great work! | Stop that! |
| Thanks for helping me. | You know better than that! |
| You look really good today. | Don't let me see you do that! |
| Your room looks super! | I said "NO"! |
| | I told you not to do that! |

**Neutral Interactions
(typical social talking)**

How are you?
Good morning.
Let's visit a while.
What's up?
Did you see the new video game that we got?

Providing frequent positive interactions helps increase enjoyment in the daily lives of individuals with whom we work while negative interactions decrease enjoyment and make problem behavior likely.

A third guideline is that interactions should be appropriate to the individual's communication style. To illustrate, if the person uses sign language, then we should include sign language; if the individual uses a picture-communication system, then we should include the pictures. Also, it is important that we never talk down to a person by talking to a teenager or adult in a manner that we would normally use with a child. That is, we should interact with individuals in an *age appropriate* manner.

## Evaluating Interactions in a Group

At times it is important for all individuals in a group to receive brief interactions from support staff. This is most useful during group leisure times. Examples include before supper in a residential unit and on the weekend when no formal leisure activities are planned in a group home. When interacting with a group of people, the following goals may be helpful in determining if the interactions are satisfactory.

---

**Goals for Interactions in a Group**

1) Most, and where possible *all*, individuals receive an interaction during the interaction time period

2) There should be at least some positive interactions *and* more positive than negative interactions should occur

3) *All* interactions should be appropriate

---

Generally, it is desirable for at least over half, and when feasible, *all* of the individuals to receive an interaction during the interaction time period.

In almost every situation we should interact with people we support much more positively than negatively. In the perfect situation, there would never be any negative interactions. However, perfect situations rarely exist (e.g., at times, people with developmental disabilities – like all of us – need negative feedback or to be corrected for their actions).

The general guideline for positive interactions is that: (1) there should be at least some positive interactions, and (2) there should be more positive interactions than negative interactions.

It is also important to note that most normal interactions express no specific approval or disapproval – they are simply common conversation. Most interactions observed among support staff and individuals with disabilities will not have any positive or negative features, but these types of typical social interactions are still very important for increasing individual enjoyment.

The guideline for appropriateness of staff interactions with people we support is that *all* interactions should be appropriate as defined earlier. That is, we should interact with individuals in accordance with their age.

Also, to be able to decide if interactions are appropriate, we must know what is appropriate for each individual. We must know the person's usual mode of communication.

# Defusing Potential Problem Situations with Positive Interactions

Earlier we mentioned that frequent, positive interactions can help prevent problem behavior. One way interactions prevent problem behavior is that when an individual is involved in a positive interaction with a staff person, the individual is likely to be doing something enjoyable. As a result, the individual is not likely to engage in problem behavior.

There is also another way interactions can help prevent or reduce problem behavior. Earlier we talked about the ABC model as part of positive behavior support.

To review a little bit, antecedents (the "A" part of the model) are events that occur before a behavior that make it likely the behavior will occur. Behavior is the "B" part of the model and consequences – reinforcers or punishers – the "C" part. Reinforcers increase how often a behavior occurs and punishers decrease how often a behavior occurs.

As part of positive behavior support, we try to identify antecedents to problem behavior and then remove or change those antecedents to prevent the problem behavior. That is, we try to find out what events usually come right before a problem behavior, and then change those events before the behavior occurs.

Before talking about changing antecedents to problem behavior, it is important to note a common mistake. If we wait until the problem behavior occurs and then interact or redirect the individual to a desired activity, what is likely to happen? We might actually reinforce the problem behavior by providing positive attention or desired activities right after the behavior.

One way to change antecedents to problem behavior is to interact with an individual when we see a situation that usually is followed by a problem behavior.

| ABC Model for Defusing Problem Behavior | | |
|---|---|---|
| Antecedent | Behavior | Consequence |
| upset or agitated behavior (quick arm movements, finger tapping, etc.) | aggression (hitting, biting, etc.) | provide a consequence for the *antecedent behavior* by interacting and interrupting -- the antecedent is then changed and the problem behavior that usually follows the antecedent behavior is prevented |

By interacting with the person *before* the problem behavior is likely to occur, two things happen that make it less likely there will be a problem.

•       First, we *interrupt* and change the antecedent

- Second, we *redirect* the person's attention away from the situation that is likely to lead to a problem behavior.

Remember, we can use interactions within the ABC model to make it less likely that problem behavior will occur by:

- Looking for antecedents to problem behavior

- Interacting in a positive manner with the person as soon as we see the antecedent and *before* the problem behavior occurs

- Redirecting the individual's attention to the interaction or another activity *before* the problem behavior occurs

# Module 12: Prompting

**Objectives:**                                                    **Trainee Notes**

Upon completion of this module, trainees should be able to:

(1) Identify a verbal, gestural, modeling, and physical prompt
(2) Provide prompts that are best for the individual
(3) Train steps of a skill in order using a task analysis
(4) Use a least-to-most assistive prompting strategy

# Introduction

When an individual with a developmental disability is learning a new behavior or skill, we may need to help the person to do at least part if not all of the skill at first. The help we give is called *prompting*. In the ABC model, prompts are antecedents because they come before the behavior and make the behavior more likely to occur. We will talk about ways we can prompt people to help them learn skills more quickly and easily.

There are many different types of prompts that help people learn new skills.

---

**Different Types of Prompts**

**Verbal**         a spoken question or instruction that helps
                   the learner do part or all of a skill

**Gestural**       pointing, tapping, or any other body motion
                   that helps the learner know what to do

**Modeling**       showing the learner how to do part or all of a
                   skill

**Physical**       guidance involving touch from the teacher to
                   help the learner do the skill – physical prompts
                   can range from a brief touch to complete
                   guidance whereby the teacher moves the learner
                   completely through part or all of a skill

---

A *verbal prompt* is any spoken question, instruction, or direction that helps a person perform a skill. To help Susan learn to tell staff when she is finished with her work, a verbal prompt could be to say, "Susan, press your switch to tell me you are finished."

Some verbal prompts provide less specific information than telling a person what to do. For example, we can remind Susan to press her switch by asking, "What do you do when finished with your work?"

Verbal prompts should include only as many words as needed to provide a clear direction. When a person has trouble understanding what we say, too much talking may be more confusing than helpful. It may also be helpful if we use the same words as prompts each time the skill is taught.

Another type of prompt to assist an individual in completing a skill is a *gestural prompt*. A gestural prompt involves pointing to or touching something or any other body motion by the teacher that directs the learner's attention toward what should be done next.

*Modeling* is another way to assist someone in performing a new behavior. Modeling involves showing the learner how to do a behavior or skill. Model only as much of the skill as the person can remember. Modeling can be effective with any learner but is probably most effective with people who learn relatively quickly. People with severe intellectual disabilities may not always benefit as much from modeling prompts.

*Physical* prompts involve physical guidance or touch from a teacher to assist a learner in performing a behavior. Physical prompts can range from brief touch to complete guidance involving moving the learner through all of a given behavior.

One way to vary how much help is provided by a physical prompt is by changing the place on the learner's body where the physical assistance is provided. For example, when teaching a learner who has severe movement problems to pick up a leisure material, we can begin by guiding the learner's arm toward the material. A more assistive physical prompt would be to guide the learner's wrist toward the material. The most assistive physical prompt for helping the learner to pick up a leisure material would be to place your hand over the learner's hand to guide the hand to pick up the material.

---

**Matching Prompts to the Individual Level of Helpfulness\***

| Least | | | | Most |
|-------|---|---|---|------|
| *verbal* | *gestural* | *modeling* | *partial physical guidance* | *full physical guidance* |

\*one example of how prompts can vary in helpfulness

---

Some types of prompts may be more helpful than other types of prompts to a particular learner. As a general rule, verbal and gestural prompts usually provide only a little help whereas full physical guidance provides the most help. However, which prompts are most or least helpful depends a lot on the learner receiving the prompt. For example, if the learner has very good language skills, a very light physical prompt may be less helpful than telling the person what to do. The example shown above is just one way prompts can vary in helpfulness; there are a number of other ways as well.

Some prompts are not useful at all for certain people. For example, if a person has a hearing impairment, verbal prompts will probably not be helpful. If a person becomes upset when touched or physically guided to do something, using physical prompts may not be a good idea.

The types of prompts used with each learner must be used with the individual learner in mind. Matching prompts to the individual will be easier if we have taken the time to get to know the person before trying to teach. We will talk more about how to provide prompts. However, first we will discuss how to look at a skill that we want to teach so that we will know exactly what we want to prompt when teaching a learner.

# Task Analysis

Often, a skill we may be teaching will include many different behaviors that a learner has to do to complete the skill. For example, a skill like throwing a paper cup away after a coffee break can be described as a series of actions or behaviors.

---

**Task Analysis for Throwing a Paper Cup Away after Coffee Break**

1. Pick up cup from table

2. Walk to trash can

3. Throw cup in trash can

4. Return to seat at table

---

Task analyzing a skill that involves many behaviors and then teaching the skill as a series of small steps makes the skill easier to learn. Task analysis makes the skill easier to learn in two ways.

*One way task analysis makes a skill easier to learn is that it describes the steps of a skill so that the skill is taught the same way every time.* Teaching someone to do a skill the same way every time helps the person to learn the skill more quickly.

*Teaching a skill by keeping the steps in the same order every time we teach the skill makes the skill easier to learn because each step is a signal for the next step in the task analysis.* Writing down a task analysis helps us teach a skill the same way every time with all the steps in the same order.

# When Task Analyses Are Not Needed

Not all skills need to be taught using a task analysis. For example, if LaShonda already knows how to wipe her face with a napkin but just does not use the skill at meal or snack time to keep her face clean, we would not need a task analysis to teach this skill. Because LaShonda already knows how to wipe her face, we would simply prompt her when it is time to wipe her face and then reinforce the face wiping. Teaching someone *when* to use a skill that the person already knows how to do does not require a task analysis.

A task analysis also would not be needed when teaching someone to perform a skill more quickly or for a longer period of time. For example, teaching Carlos to work on his job for longer periods of time without a break is not the type of skill that needs to be task analyzed because he already knows how to do the job. Instead, we would increase the amount of Carlos' work little by little and reinforce his work with praise and break time when he completes all his work.

Again, task analysis is useful when we are teaching a person to do a skill that the person does not already know how to do correctly.

## Least-to-Most Assistive Prompting

To help someone learn a skill that has been task analyzed, we should provide prompts following a simple guideline. *We never provide more help than someone needs to perform a skill.*

When teaching a skill for the first time, we must find out how much help the learner needs for each step of the task analysis. We begin by allowing the learner to try each step of the task analysis without help. If the learner does not do the step, we provide a mild prompt such as a verbal prompt. If the learner cannot do the step after the verbal prompt, we give a more helpful prompt like a gestural or modeling prompt. If the learner does not do the step after these prompts, we give a more helpful prompt such as a partial physical prompt. If a partial physical prompt does not help the learner enough to do the step, we would give even more help such as by guiding the learner completely through the step (full physical prompt).

It is important to remember that physical prompting is *not* forcing the person to do something. It is a guide and not used if the person actively resists.

# Prompt Fading

Once we know how much help someone needs to do each step of the skill, then each time a person practices the skill, we begin *each step* by giving less help than the person usually needs to do the step. If the first prompt is not enough help to complete a step, we give more and more helpful prompts until the person does a step correctly. As a step is done correctly, we teach the next step in the task analysis the same way.

Using prompts in the way just described is called a *least-to-most assistive prompting strategy*. In a least-to-most assistive prompting strategy, a learner should never get more help than is needed to complete any step of the task analysis. Prompting is reduced as less and less helpful prompts are needed and the learner does more and more of the steps without any help. The process of reducing prompts in this way is called *prompt fading*. The goal is for a learner to learn to perform all the steps of a skill without trainer prompting.

# Avoiding Common Prompting Mistakes

---

**Most Common Mistakes Using**
**Least-to-Most Assistive Prompting**

1. Providing the same prompt more than one time on a given step (repeating prompts).

2. Providing a more helpful prompt too quickly without giving the learner time to respond.

3. Providing full physical guidance the first time a learner tries a step.

---

There are some common mistakes often made when learning to use a least-to-most assistive prompting strategy. One common mistake is that we repeat the same prompt on a given step rather than giving more helpful prompts when a learner does not complete a step (e.g., "Throw your cup and napkin away", "Come on, you can do it", "Can you throw your cup and napkin away?" etc.).

Repeating prompts for a given step only makes the teaching process longer and confuses the learner. Also, instructions and prompting may be disliked by some learners and providing too many instructions can lead to behavior problems.

A second prompting mistake is prompting too quickly. Remember to wait at least a few seconds between each prompt to give the learner time to respond to a prompt. Sometimes we give a more assistive prompt without allowing enough time for the learner to respond to a less helpful prompt.

A third prompting mistake is using full physical guidance as the first prompt on any step of the task analysis. If full physical guidance is given as the first prompt for a step, the learner has no chance to complete any part of the step without help.

Teaching involves not only following a task analysis, prompting and providing reinforcement but also correcting learner errors when they make errors during teaching. Because all of these skills are necessary for good teaching, the skills check for teaching skills will be conducted after the next module on error correction is taught.

# Module 13: Error Correction

**Objectives:**                                                    **Trainee Notes**

Upon completion of this module, trainees should be able to:

(1) Demonstrate appropriate error correction
(2) Conduct a teaching session with correct use of prompts, error correction, and positive reinforcement
(3) Critically observe another person's teaching while completing a checklist

## Error Correction in Teaching New Skills

Maybe your grandmother said, "You learn from your mistakes". That may be true in many cases. However, when people are learning a new skill, making many mistakes or errors often slows learning. Because it is important to reduce the mistakes or errors a person makes while learning a new skill, we will talk about how to correct learner errors during teaching.

## When to Use Prompting versus When to Use Error Correction

Sometimes people get confused about when to use prompting and when to use error correction. Remember the ABC model (**A**ntecedents, **B**ehavior, **C**onsequences)? Prompts are antecedents because they occur before the desired behavior, to make the behavior more likely to occur.

---

**Use prompting**

...when a learner does not do anything when instructed

**Use error correction**

...when a learner does the wrong thing when instructed

---

When a learner is asked to wipe his mouth with a napkin, if the person does nothing (does not respond to the verbal prompt), we provide more helpful prompts until the behavior occurs.

An *error* is when a learner does the wrong thing. Based on the ABC model, error correction is the consequence we use after the learner makes a mistake.

For example, when instructed to wipe his mouth, if the learner tosses the napkin on the floor, *then tossing the napkin is an error.* We use an error correction procedure when the napkin is tossed.

Again, prompts are used *before* the desired behavior; error correction is used *after* a learner does the wrong behavior. However, our actions used to prompt or correct an error may be the same – they just occur at different times related to the learner's behavior.

# Error Prevention

If possible, we should try to prevent errors from occurring so that we do not have to use error correction. If we see that the learner is about to make a mistake, we should increase assistance (give a more helpful prompt) to prevent the error.

---

**Error Correction**

1. Stop the error in a manner appropriate to the learner

2. Repeat the part of the skill where the error was made

3. Provide as much help as the learner needs to complete the part of the skill where the error was made without making another error

---

The reason for using a more helpful prompt to guide the learner after an error is made is that we do not want the person to make the same mistake again during the teaching session. When learners make the same mistakes over and over, they are practicing the skill the wrong way. The more they practice the error, the more likely they are to learn the skill the wrong way. Also, for many people with developmental disabilities, and especially those with autism, it can be very hard to help them change how they do something after they have done it a certain way.

# Common Mistakes Made with Error Correction

When a learner makes an error during a teaching session, common mistakes made during teaching include:

- Not correcting an error made by the person

- Giving a prompt during the learner's second attempt that is not helpful enough to prevent a second error on the same step

# Module 14: Naturalistic Teaching

## Objectives:                                    **Trainee Notes**

Upon completion of this module, trainees should be able to:

(1) Describe naturalistic teaching
(2) Demonstrate naturalistic teaching
(3) Identify good opportunities to do naturalistic teaching
     as part of routine, daily activities
(4) Describe three advantages of naturalistic teaching

## Naturalistic Teaching

Our discussion on teaching has focused on working 1:1 with a person with a developmental disability for the main purpose of teaching a meaningful skill to the person. This often means carrying out a formal, written teaching plan with the person. The teaching involves following the steps of a task analysis, prompting, correcting errors, and reinforcement.

Although formal teaching in the way we have been talking about is very important, it is not the only way to teach. Also, there are limits to how much time we have to work 1:1 with a person we support to carry out formal teaching sessions. We must look for more ways to teach during the routine day to help people with disabilities become more independent. One of the best ways is to teach *naturalistically*.

---

**Naturalistic Teaching:**

including brief instruction within ongoing activities

---

*Naturalistic teaching* involves including brief instruction within ongoing activities of the people we support. Naturalistic teaching focuses on teaching a meaningful skill to a person with a disability *at the exact moment the skill is needed* and in the situation the skill is needed.

 Can you think of examples of naturalistic teaching with which you are familiar?

There are two main parts to naturalistic teaching. The first part is using basic teaching procedures that we have talked about in an *on-the-spot* manner during a routinely occurring activity with someone we support. The second is recognizing good opportunities to teach that arise naturally during daily activities. First we will talk about how to use the teaching procedures in a naturalistic way.

## Using Basic Teaching Procedures Naturalistically During the Day

A good way to think about naturalistic teaching is with the *SWAWT Model* (pronounced SWAT).

---

## SWAWT Model of Naturalistic Teaching

**S:** *Say* what to do (verbal prompt)

**W:** *Wait* and *Watch*

**A:** *Act out* (model or gestural prompt)

**W:** *Wait* and *Watch*

**T:** *Touch* to guide (physical prompt)

*. . . and always reinforce the learner's completion
of what was prompted*

---

*SWAWT* was developed as a way to remind staff working with people with developmental disabilities to provide brief instruction during ongoing activities. The **S** stands for "say", which is when we provide a verbal prompt for someone we support to do something. The **W** stands for "wait and watch", which means we give the person time to respond to the verbal prompt and watch to see what the person does. If the person does what was prompted, we then praise or otherwise reinforce the person's action.

If the person does not respond to the verbal prompt, then we act out (the **A** part) by either modeling or gesturing. We then wait and watch again (**W**). Just as before, if the person does what was prompted, we reinforce. If not, we carry out the **T** which stands for "touch to guide". That is, we provide as much physical assistance (physical prompt) as the person needs to complete the action and then reinforce. However, we do not force the person to do something, we only provide assistance through teaching.

See how *SWAWT* involves least-to-most assistive prompting and reinforcement as we practiced in previous classes? Going from **S**ay (verbal prompt) to the **A**ct out (model or gestural prompt) if necessary and then to the **T**ouch to guide (physical prompt) if necessary is a type of least-to-most prompting . . . and we always reinforce the person's completion of the action.

Error correction can also be used if the person makes an error by doing something other than what was prompted. Usually with naturalistic teaching the error correction involves the **T**ouch to guide part of *SWAWT*, through which we provide as much physical prompting as necessary to help the person complete the action. Again, we do not force the person's movements; we just provide assistance.

Notice that naturalistic teaching in this manner does not include a task analysis – for several reasons. First, because naturalistic teaching occurs on-the-spot without prior planning, a task analysis would not be available. Second, naturalistic teaching is designed for skills that involve only one or very few behaviors, such that a task analysis is usually not needed anyway.

This was the case with our previous demonstration in class of using naturalistic teaching to teach a person with a developmental disability to open a bottle of water. The skill only involved twisting the cap off the bottle.

# Recognizing Opportunities to Teach During Daily Activities

The second part of naturalistic teaching as noted earlier is *recognizing opportunities to teach* during ongoing, daily activities. We should look for as many opportunities to teach as possible during daily activities. Below are some of the most important types of opportunities.

---

**Important Opportunities to Teach Naturalistically**

When we are about to do something for a person with a disability . . . instead, teach the person to do it

When a person we support wants help to do something . . . instead of helping by doing the task for the person, help by teaching the person to do it

A situation in which a person we support has had problem behavior in the past . . . teach the person a functional replacement behavior *before* the problem behavior occurs

---

The first important opportunity is when we as staff are about to do something for a person whom we support that involves only a few behaviors to complete the action. Instead of doing the task for the person, we should remember *SWAWT* and use the opportunity to teach the person to do the task.

We often do things for people we support because it is a nice thing to do. This is one important type of support. However, in the long run, it is usually much nicer to teach the person to do it for him or herself. In this way, the person with a disability will not be dependent on us or others to have the action completed in the future. The person will be able to do it whenever needed or desired.

A second important opportunity for teaching is when a person wants help to do something. Instead of doing it for the person, remember SWAWT and teach the person right then to do it.

In other cases the people we support might specifically ask for our help to do something. If what is being asked involves only one or a few behaviors to accomplish, these situations also represent a good opportunity to use naturalistic teaching to teach the person to do the task at that moment.

A third type of teaching opportunity is a situation in which a person we support has had problem behavior in the past. Before the problem behavior occurs we can teach or prompt a replacement behavior that is appropriate and serves the same purpose as the problem behavior. For example, a natural time to teach Regina to ask for help with a task rather than throw a tantrum when she does not know how to do the task is when she appears to need help. We observe for signs that she needs help and teach her to ask for help *before* she begins to tantrum.

Naturalistic teaching can be very helpful for the people we support in several ways.

| ? | Can you think of some advantages of naturalistic teaching? |

> **Advantages of Naturalistic Teaching**
>
> Provides many ways to promote independence by teaching skills at the moment they are needed and in the situation they are needed
>
> Well-suited for integrated, community settings
>
> It is applied when the people we support are often highly motivated to learn

One of the most important advantages of naturalistic teaching is that it gives us many ways to help the people we support learn new skills and increase their independence. By increasing their independence, they can do more things on their own that they need or want to do, and do those things when they want to do them – they do not have to wait on staff or others. In this way their daily routines can become much more enjoyable for them.

A second advantage of naturalistic teaching is that it works well for promoting independence of people with developmental disabilities in integrated, community settings. Naturalistic teaching can be incorporated within many community situations.

For example, a person wants to use the ice machine at a convenience store to put ice in a soda cup. However, she does not know how to use the ice machine. We could use the *SWAWT* approach to teach her how to hold the cup under the machine and push the ice lever. Or, if a person wants to enter a park but does not know how to open the latch on the park gate we could teach at that moment how to lift the latch and push open the gate.

Naturalistic teaching works well in community settings because it requires only a few minutes at most to carry out. Therefore it does not interfere with the ongoing activity. Also, it can be done without drawing unnecessary attention to the person with a disability.

Another important advantage is that the person we support is often highly motivated to have some action completed. Again, this was represented with the earlier demonstration we did in class of teaching a person to open a water bottle. Because the person wanted the bottle opened at that time (remember how she held the bottle in front of the trainer to indicate she wanted the trainer to open it), the person was motivated to respond to the helpful prompts the trainer provided in order to complete the task.

# Module 15: Program Implementation

## Objectives:                                           **Trainee Notes**

Upon completion of this module, trainees should be able to:

(1) Describe how directions for implementing Behavior Support
    Plans (BSPs) must be followed as written
(2) Identify the basic parts in a BSP that are needed to carry
    out the BSP

## Importance of Following Directions for Implementing Behavior Support Plans

A very important part of positive behavior support is implementing Behavior Support Plans (BSPs). Every support staff who interacts with a person with a developmental disability must know what is in the person's BSP. Every support staff must also follow the directions for implementing the BSP *exactly as the program is written.*

---

Basic Rule for Using Behavior Support Plans:
the plans ***must*** be carried out as written

---

Following the directions for BSPs is important for making sure each person we work with gets the supports that the person is supposed to get. Carefully following directions for BSPs is also important for being able to tell if the BSP is working. If directions are not followed, then we cannot tell if the program works or not. Carrying out BSPs is part of almost every support staffs' job every day.

# Guidelines for Following Behavior Support Plan Directions

In order to carry out a BSP, one must be able to understand and follow the directions for the programs. Because programs can be written in many ways, the programs must be carefully read. There are four guidelines that can be helpful in making sure one follows the directions for each BSP.

---

## Guidelines for Following Behavior Support Plan Directions

**Preventive steps**

What things should be in place in the person's environment?

What things should not be present in the person's environment?

**Antecedents**

What is likely to happen right before a problem behavior?

What should you do if an event happens that usually comes right before a problem behavior, or how can things be changed so the event does not happen?

**Behavior**

What are the target behaviors to decrease?

What are the target behaviors to increase?

**Consequences**

What should you do if the person does the behaviors that are to be decreased?

What should you do if the person does the behaviors that are to be increased?

---

When reading a BSP, it is helpful to keep in mind the ABC model of positive behavior support. Remember:

- **A** is the Antecedents -- those events that come before a behavior (and make it likely the behavior will occur)

- **B** is the behavior of concern

- **C** is the consequence to the behavior (what happens right after the behavior).

Most BSPs have information about the A, the B, and the C. One should look for each of these parts of every BSP to help understand how to carry out the program.

There is one other part of many BSPs to look for: *preventive steps*. Preventive steps are those things that should be in place in the location in which the person lives, works, or plays. Often the preventive steps relate to setting events that affect the antecedents and consequences for problem behavior as we discussed in an earlier class. Preventive steps can be any number of things, and are usually planned to be in place to help prevent the problem behavior from occurring. Preventive steps are often found in the *Prevention* part of BSPs.

---

**Examples of Preventive Steps**

1. Make sure Juan always has his picture cards with him

2. Help Sharyn avoid crowds and loud noises

3. Tyrone should always have access to his favorite wallet

4. Lou should never be alone with Chi

---

The first example is for people with developmental disabilities who use devices to communicate. These may be pictures, talking devices, word cards, or whatever else may be part of the person's support plan. If the people we support do not have their usual means of communicating, they may use problem behavior to communicate their wants and needs.

The second example is for people with developmental disabilities who do not like crowds or loud noises. This is often the case for people who have autism. When some people we support are in crowded or loud places, they become confused, scared, or simply upset. Support staff must try to help these individuals avoid these types of places so that problem behavior does not occur.

The third example is for people with developmental disabilities who are more satisfied – and as such, less likely to show problem behavior – when they have a favorite item close at hand. Think about your behavior if you did not have a favorite item close at hand (e.g., phone, purse, wallet).

The fourth example is for a person we support who is likely to act out against a certain peer. Support staff should know whom the person is likely to act out against and make sure the person is never left alone with that peer.

There are many more types of preventive steps that are often in BSPs. Support staff must be very familiar with these and make sure they are in place as written in the BSP.

Some BSPs are written more clearly than others. It is important to carefully read each BSP to make sure we know exactly what to do in order to carry out the program. If we cannot decide what should be done, we should ask whoever wrote the program or a supervisor what to do.

Sometimes not all of the parts of BSP directions that we list as guidelines for what to look for will be present in the BSP. For example, sometimes it is not known what happens just before a problem behavior (the antecedents), so there is no information about antecedents in the BSP.

In other cases, the specific behavior to increase is not always clear. In these cases, the opposite of the behavior to decrease – or simply the absence of the behavior to decrease – is what we want to increase. For example, for someone who shows head-hitting, we might increase any useful behavior other than head-hitting such as a work or leisure activity that involves the appropriate use of the hands.

If we are still not sure about some of the BSP directions even when we use the guidelines (e.g., we cannot find answers to the questions in the guidelines), we should always ask for help.

# Module 16: Problem Solving

**Objectives:**

Upon completion of this module, trainees should be able to:

(1) Describe five situations in which to ask for help
     in carrying out a Behavior Support Plan (BSP)

## Review of Importance of Following Directions for Implementing Behavior Support Plans

A key point of our last class session was that Behavior Support Plans (BSPs) must be carried out exactly as the plans are written.

---

**Basic Rule for Using Behavior Support Plans:**
The plans *must* be carried out as written

---

In short, plans must be carried out exactly as written so people with developmental disabilities can get the supports they are supposed to get, and so we can evaluate if the plans are working.

# When to Ask for Help
# with Behavior Support Plans

As we talked about in the last class, at times questions come up when carrying out BSPs. It is important to know when to ask for help from your supervisor or from someone who wrote the BSP. In this class we will discuss the most important times when to ask for help about a BSP.

---

**When to Ask for Help with Behavior Support Plans**

1. When you are not sure how to carry out the plan

2. When problem behavior results from carrying out the plan

3. If someone is likely to be hurt when the plan is carried out

4. When the plan is carried out and the behavior does not get better -- or even gets worse

5. When you cannot carry out the plan because of other duties

---

The first situation in which we should ask for help is when we cannot understand how to carry out parts of the plan. As noted before, BSPs are written in many ways, and some ways are easier to understand than others. If we do not understand part of the plan, we cannot carry it out correctly.

The second situation to ask for help is when it appears that a person who has a BSP has problems when the plan is carried out.

Sometimes plans do not have the effect that the plans are supposed to have. For example, a person we support may find parts of the plan very unpleasant, and react with a new type of problem behavior. If it appears a person really does not like parts of the plan, or shows serious problem behavior when the plan is carried out, this information should be given to the supervisor or someone who wrote the plan. In some of these cases, the plan may have to be changed.

Another, and related, time when it is important to ask for help with a BSP is if it looks like someone may be hurt due to how the plan is carried out. If a person with a disability, or *anyone* else, seems to be at risk of harm when the program is carried out, then this information should be given to a supervisor or someone who wrote the plan right away.

A fourth situation in which to ask for help with a BSP is when the plan does not seem to be working. That is, after the plan has been used, the behavior of the person with a developmental disability does not get better, or even gets worse. At these times, support team members need to know that the plan does not seem to be working.

This is one reason we take data on behavior of people we support – to tell if the behavior is getting better or worse. Sometimes though, we need to help make sure that people who write the plans know that the data show that the plan does not seem to be working.

Also, sometimes the data show that the plan may be working but there is other information that may show the plan has some problems. For example, a plan might be carried out to decrease how often self-injury such as head hitting occurs. The data that is collected may show a decrease in head hitting but a staff person sees that even though head hitting occurs less often, when it does happen it is much more serious than before (e.g., the head hits are much harder than they used to be).

In short, when the plan is not working even though it is carried out in the right way, this information needs to be shared with a supervisor or someone who wrote the plan.

Another time to ask for help is when we find that we truly cannot carry out the plan. For example, in some cases the plan cannot be carried out because there are not enough staff present to do everything that needs to be done.

There are many reasons why this type of situation can occur, such as trying to carry out BSPs for many people with developmental disabilities at the same time, staff absences, breakdowns in scheduled activities, etc. If in fact a plan cannot be carried out, then this information needs to be shared with a supervisor right away. The individual's support team can then work on fixing the situation.

# Module 17: Functional Assessment

**Objectives:**                                                    **Trainee Notes**

Upon completion of this module, trainees should be able to:

(1) Describe a functional assessment
(2) Describe how problem behavior is a type of communication
(3) Describe two main functions of problem behavior

## Review of ABC Model

We have talked a lot about the ABC model of positive behavior support. We have talked about how to define and observe the "B" – the person's behavior of concern. We have also talked about observing the "A" – antecedents. Finally, we have talked about the "C" – consequences, and how consequences can increase behavior through reinforcement and decrease behavior through punishment.

In this class we will talk about another way to see how behavior is increased or decreased as a result of the consequences to the behavior. This time however, we will look at behavior more from the point of view of the person we support.

Looking at why a person with a developmental disability does something from the person's view is an important part of the person-centered value of positive behavior support; we want to know what problem behavior does for the person.

We can look at what problem behavior does for a person through a process called *functional assessment.* Using a functional assessment, we assess what *function* or purpose a problem behavior serves for a person. A functional assessment tells us what a person gets, or gets out of, by doing a certain behavior.

---

**Functional Assessment:**

a process to determine what purpose
or function problem behavior serves for a person

---

A functional assessment is a very good way to find out what the consequence is for a person we support doing a behavior. Remember that people do things because their behavior is reinforced. The reinforcement may be positive in that a person gets something desired by doing a behavior. The reinforcement may also be negative in that the behavior stops something the person does not want.

By using a functional assessment to tell if a person uses a problem behavior to get something that is wanted, or stop something that is not wanted, we can begin to understand the person's motivation for the problem behavior. Behavior Support Plans (BSPs) that address problem behavior should always be based on some type of functional assessment.

# Types of Functional Assessments

There are different ways to do a functional assessment. Typically you will not be asked to do a functional assessment by yourself. A functional assessment is usually done by a group of support team members. Often a behavior specialist, behavior analyst, psychologist, or someone else with a lot of training in positive behavior support will take the lead in doing a functional assessment.

You may, however, be expected to help with a functional assessment. Our concern here is that you know what a functional assessment is and how it can be used to understand a person's motivation for a problem behavior. When we understand the person's motivation for a problem behavior, then we are more likely to have a good BSP to help the person overcome the problem.

---

**Types of Functional Assessments**

1. Interview
2. Direct observation
3. Analog functional analysis

---

One type of functional assessment is to ask specific questions of people who know a person with a developmental disability about situations in which the person is most and least likely to have a problem behavior. Questions are also asked about what the person appears to get, or get out of, when the behavior occurs. These types of questions make up what is called an *interview* functional assessment.

Another type of a functional assessment is to *observe* a person's problem behavior in different activities during the day (and across days). During the observations, what happens right before (i.e., the antecedent) and after (the consequence) the behavior occurs is usually recorded (A-B-C data collection). This type of functional assessment is called *direct observation*. You may be asked to help collect data on the problem behavior of a person you support.

A different type of a functional assessment involves doing certain activities with a person we support and see how the person reacts to the activities. This way is called an *analog functional analysis* because we create activities, or *analogs*, for the person. The purpose is to see in which type of situations the problem behavior is most and least likely to occur.

The analog functional analysis is different from an observational assessment in that one creates activities or analogs, whereas the other involves observations during naturally occurring activities in the day of the person we support.

In some cases, the analogs created in an analog functional analysis may actually cause problem behavior to occur. Therefore, these types of functional assessments must be done carefully by someone with advanced training in positive behavior support and with appropriate protections and approvals.

Whether a functional assessment includes just interviews and observations or also includes an analog analysis, the purpose is the same: to help determine what function or purpose the behavior serves for the person.

Again, we use a functional assessment to tell us:

• what the person's behavior gets for the person – that is, what the person wants and/or

• what the person gets stopped or gets away from – something the person does not want

We will talk about both of these *functions* of problem behavior.

## When Problem Behavior Functions to Get a Person Something the Person Wants

Think about a person with a disability who puts his face very close to a staff member's face and then talks using dirty language. When the person interacts in this way, we observe that the staff member always says something to the person.

To help decide what a person's behavior may get for the individual, it can be useful to ask, "What is the person's behavior telling us?" In almost every case, problem behavior is a way for someone to tell us something; the problem behavior serves a *communication function* or purpose for the person with a developmental disability.

111

Problem behavior can function to get a person many things the person wants. A person might take a peer's dessert because the person wants the dessert. A person might take off her clothes because she likes the close attention she gets when someone helps put her clothes back on.

## When Problem Behavior Functions to Let a Person Stop Something That the Person Does Not Want

Think about a person with a developmental disability who tries to hit or slap a support staff when the support staff starts to help the person do a certain activity such as put his dishes by the sink after dinner. When the person begins to hit or slap, the support staff tells him to "Never mind!" and leaves him alone.

| ? | Does the person's hitting or slapping behavior help him get out of something that he does not want to do at times? What might he be getting out of? |
|---|---|

To decide what a person's problem behavior helps him get out of, it can be helpful to ask the same question we talked about earlier: "What is the person's behavior telling us?". Again, problem behavior is almost always a way for someone we support to tell us something. In the case just noted, the behavior tells us he does not want to do what someone is asking or telling him to do.

---

### Practice Identifying the Function of Behavior

In the following scenarios, what might each person be getting or getting out of by engaging in the problem behavior:

1. Laura lives in a group home with three other people. At supper time, all four persons go to the table. When a staff member begins giving one of Laura's peers a serving of food before serving her, she begins to scream and pull her own hair. The staff member then quickly gives Laura a food serving, and Laura calms down.

2. Jefferson has a supported job in a printing company, in which he does several job tasks. When he is given the task of folding mailing fliers, which he knows how to do, he always tears the fliers. When he begins to tear the fliers, that task is removed from him.

---

Remember in an earlier class we talked about *replacement skills*. Teaching replacement skills allows a person we support to use an appropriate behavior to get something wanted or to indicate something is not wanted. Teaching functional replacement skills, such as by teaching a person to say or sign that s/he wants something rather than to use problem behavior to get what is wanted, is a very good way to prevent problem behavior from occurring.

# Module 18: Data Collection

**Objectives:**

Upon completion of this module, trainees should be able to:

(1) Identify and collect frequency data
(2) Identify and collect interval data
(3) Identify and collect duration data

## The Importance of Data

In an earlier class we talked about the importance of focusing on *behavior* as a key part of positive behavior support. To briefly review, *behavior refers to anything a person does*. A person's behavior should be described so that it can be observed and measured. Most importantly, the behavior should be described in enough detail so that people can easily agree when the behavior occurs.

In positive behavior support, we collect data on one or more of the following types of behavior:

•      skills that are being taught

•      desirable behaviors to increase

•      problem behaviors to decrease

*Data* on behavior are almost as important as the behavior itself. Almost every agency providing supports for people with disabilities requires the collection of data on the behavior of the people they support. Data that provide information about the behavior, and particularly how often the behavior occurs, are also a critical part of positive behavior support.

There are many reasons for collecting data on behavior. However, there are two most important reasons.

---

**Why Collect Data on Behavior**

Data help us understand why certain behaviors
occur and do not occur

Data allow us to determine if our support programs
are working or not

---

First, collecting data on behavior helps us understand why a behavior occurs or does not occur; *data can provide information about the situations in which a person is most and least likely to do something.*

We can use information about why a behavior occurs to help people we support do things that are beneficial and enjoyable, and not to do things that result in problems.

The second reason for collecting data on behavior is that the data allow us to evaluate whether the behavior is getting better or worse. This is the reason we will focus on in this class.

Data are especially useful for deciding if certain behaviors are occurring more or less often. This information is important to evaluate if our efforts to teach useful skills and reduce problem behavior are working. Generally, this type of data indicates whether we should keep doing what we are doing to support someone (when the data indicate the behavior is getting better), or whether we should change what we are doing (the data indicate the behavior is not getting better).

Because of the importance of data as part of positive behavior support, we must be able to determine *how* to collect data on important behavior, then accurately *collect* the data and finally, *make sense of the data* for use in our support efforts.

There are many ways to collect three main types of data:

- Frequency recording

- Interval recording

- Duration recording

The specific way to collect data in each situation must be based on the information that needs to be collected, as well as how practical it is to collect various types of data in your own setting. Usually, the person who writes the Behavior Support Plan (BSP) will include information on the data to be collected.

One way to make data collection easier is to use prepared forms for data collection. We will demonstrate and practice collecting data and using several data collection forms in this session.

# Types of Data and Data Collection I:
# Frequency Recording

The most common type of data collected in support settings for people with disabilities is usually through *frequency recording*. Frequency recording means that we simply record when an event – or *behavior* – occurs.

By making a record of each time we see a certain behavior, we can count the number of times a behavior occurs. Such a record tells us the *frequency* of the behavior.

Frequency recording can be used with many behaviors. However, this type of data collection is easiest to use when it is very clear when the behavior begins and ends. In order to know when a behavior begins and ends, the behavior must be defined very clearly. This is one of the reasons we must carefully define certain behaviors of people we support as we just talked about.

Which behaviors we decide to count with frequency recording depends on the behaviors that we would like people we support to do more or less often. To illustrate, if we want to support a person with a developmental disability in completing a job task, we would need to count how many times the person did the task.

We can also use frequency recording for behavior that we would like to see decrease.

# Types of Data and Data Collection II: Interval Recording

Frequency recording can be used with many types of behavior. However, it is sometimes not practical to count every time a certain behavior occurs. In some cases, a behavior may occur very quickly and many times. For example, some types of self-injurious behavior such as face slapping may occur 20 or more times a minute. This makes it difficult to count each face slapping behavior.

At other times, it is not necessary to count each time a behavior occurs. Instead, we record only if the behavior occurred at all. In these types of situations, data can be collected with *interval recording*.

Interval recording is also a commonly used data collection method in positive behavior support. There are several types of interval recording procedures. The type that is generally most useful in settings for people with disabilities involves recording if a certain behavior is observed during a specific interval of time. For example, if we wanted to count "table slamming" behavior as demonstrated in class, interval recording could be used.

# Types of Data and Data Collection III: Duration Recording

In some cases, the concern with a particular behavior is not whether it occurs or not, but how long the behavior lasts when it does occur. In such cases, *duration recording* can be used to collect important data.

Some of you have probably worked with individuals who have seizures. If you have worked with people who have seizures, you know that it is important to time how long a seizure lasts – or its *duration.* This is an example of duration recording.

Duration recording can be a useful part of positive behavior support. Sometimes we want behavior to last for longer periods of time and sometimes we want it to last for shorter periods of time.

For example, we might want to help a person we support learn to work on a clerical job task for longer periods of time before becoming tired or upset. This would help the person to obtain a supported job. Duration recording (that is, recording how long the person works before showing tired or upset types of behavior) can be helpful to determine if our support plan is effective in helping the person to work for longer periods of time.

# Deciding the Type of Data to Collect

As we have seen, there are a number of different types of data that can be useful in positive behavior support. Deciding which type of data to collect depends on each individual situation. Often support teams must meet and jointly decide the best type of data to collect. The following guidelines can be helpful in making such decisions.

---

**Guidelines for Deciding What Data to Collect**

Collect data that provide the specific type
of information needed
*and*
that can be collected with the resources at hand

---

The primary guideline for deciding the type of data to collect is what information is most important to learn. Often the decision can be made by reviewing whether it is most important to know:

1.     How many times the behavior occurred during a certain period (which would make frequency recording a good choice).

2.     If the behavior simply occurred or not during a given time period (interval recording).

3.     How long the behavior occurred (duration recording).

Sometimes it is important to know several of these things, such that more than one type of data will need to be collected.

The second guideline is more of a practical one. Specifically, the data collection method chosen *must be able to be used in light of the resources and available time for collecting data.*

In many cases, it will not be likely that certain behavior of a person we support could be counted all day long. In such cases, the day might be broken into half-hour intervals with records kept on the number of the intervals in which the behavior was observed to occur or not (interval recording) without having to count every instance of the behavior.

In other cases, it might be possible to select certain times of the day when the behavior is of special interest, and then observe the behavior during those times.

At this point it is important to note that in general, *the best data collection approach is the one that provides the needed information with the least amount of time and effort to use.*

# Module 19: Data Analysis

**Objectives:**                                                    **Trainee Notes**

Upon completion of this module, trainees should be able to:

(1) Describe importance of graphing for data analysis
(2) Use a line graph to tell if a behavior is occurring more or less often

## Review of Importance of Data

Previously we talked about the importance of collecting data on behavior of the people we support. To briefly review, we collect data to help understand why certain behaviors occur, and to evaluate if our programs are working to help change behavior. We also practiced collecting different types of data on behavior.

In this class session, we will talk about ways to make sense out of the data we collect to determine if a behavior is increasing or decreasing over time.

## Using Graphs to Make Sense Out of Data

The best way to make sense out of data collected on behavior of people we support is to *graph* the data. Graphs give us a way to see how behavior is changing over time, and whether the behavior is getting better, worse, or not changing. The purpose of this class session is to describe how to look at data on a basic line graph in order to make sense out of the data.

During the class, you will receive several handouts showing examples of graphs and we will practice interpreting the information presented on the graph. It will be important to put the handouts you receive during class in this Resource Guide. The information in this module can best be understood by reviewing the information and looking at the examples. It will also be important to include the handouts in the Resource Guide for future reference.

## The Three Basic Parts of a Graph

There are many types of graphs. We will talk about the most useful types for deciding if a behavior is occurring more or less often. Specifically, we will be talking about *line graphs.*

All line graphs have three basic parts. These are the bottom axis, the side axis, and the data itself. (Please refer to the examples of graphs handed out during class to see each of the basic parts.) The names of these parts are not that important; what is important is to be able to see and make sense out of these parts.

- The bottom axis shows periods of time in which the data were collected. This may be hours, days, weeks, months, etc.

- The side axis shows the behavior summary. The behavior summary comes from the summary section of data collection sheets that we practiced using in an earlier class. The behavior summary may be number of times the behavior occurred, percentage of observation intervals in which the behavior occurred, etc.

•      The data itself is simply where we put a point that represents the behavior summary (side axis) for a certain time period (bottom axis). We connect data points for each time period that we have a behavior summary to make a graph.

Remember when we practiced collecting data with frequency recording? Remember also that frequency recording is sometimes called frequency counts. With frequency recording, or frequency counts, we counted how often a behavior occurred during a set period of time. A graph could show how often the behavior occurred (based on the frequency counts) for each observation time period.

Another type of data collection that we practiced was interval recording. With interval recording, we recorded whether or not a certain behavior occurred during any time in the interval. The interval could be any amount of time that we thought was important for keeping track of the behavior. A graph might show the percentage of observation intervals in which the behavior occurred for a certain time period.

Graphs can show us a lot of information about a person's behavior. One of the most important reasons we use graphs is to tell if a behavior is getting better, worse, or not changing – that is, is the behavior occurring more or less often over time or not changing? In order to use a graph to answer this question, it is

125

useful to keep a basic rule in mind for making sense out of data on a graph.

---

### Basic Rule for Making Sense Out of Data on a Graph

There must be at least three data points to tell if there is a trend for the behavior to increase or decrease

---

We cannot tell from a graph if a behavior is occurring more or less often over time unless we have at least three data points on a graph. If we have not collected enough data to put three data points on a graph, then we would need to collect more data until we had at least three data points.

However, three data points are not always enough to tell if a behavior is occurring more or less often; three data points are only the least amount necessary to decide. Often we have to have more than three data points – but we always have to have at least three.

# Module 20: Scatter Plot Data Analysis

**Objective:**                                      **Trainee Notes**

Upon completion of this module, trainees should be able to:

1) Describe data shown on a basic scatter plot

## Scatter Plot Data Analysis

One of the most useful means of collecting data in order to help understand why a behavior occurs is a *scatter plot*. A scatter plot allows us to collect data in a way that shows the times and situations in which a behavior is most and least likely to occur. A scatter plot can help us understand *why* behavior occurs.

As with the previous module, it will be important to put handouts showing examples of scatter plots that you receive in this class session into this Resource Guide.

With a scatter plot, we record when a behavior occurs during many intervals over time. In this manner, a scatter plot involves interval recording as we described previously. We use a scatter plot to find out what times a behavior is most and least likely to occur. Then we study those times to see if we can find out what is going on during that time period that may lead to, or not lead to, the behavior.

When we find out when the behavior is most and least likely to occur, we would need to observe during these times to see if we can get some idea what is happening during those time periods that is affecting the behavior.

Scatter plots do not tell us for sure what is causing a behavior to occur but rather, give us some ideas that we can then think about. These ideas can help people develop useful BSPs. Scatter plots should be discussed with the support team of the person with a developmental disability and the people who write BSPs.

Again, scatter plots are best used to discuss the behavior of a person we support with members of the person's support team. We use scatter plots to:

- tell when a behavior is most and least likely to occur

- get ideas as to why the behavior occurs and does not occur in certain situations

# Module 21: Feedback

**Objectives:**                                  **Trainee Notes**

Upon completion of this module, trainees should be able to:

(1) Identify verbal feedback as a practical and effective
     means of training and motivating staff work
(2) Provide verbal feedback to a staff member following
     a 7-step protocol

# Introduction

All of us need motivation from time to time, as well as training
to help us improve our work. Supervisors can provide such
motivation and training for their staff. One of the best ways to
provide motivation and training is through feedback.

Feedback can be presented in many ways. We can give staff
feedback through formal letters, e-mails, special recognition or
awards, and by giving staff information about the progress of
the people they support.

However, the easiest and fastest way to give feedback is to
simply talk to staff about their job performance. Talking to staff
about their job performance is called *verbal* feedback. When
verbal feedback is provided often and includes the right
information, staff usually will do their jobs better and feel good
about their work.

129

If feedback is to help staff do their jobs better and feel good about their work, the feedback must be provided skillfully. In particular, feedback must make it clear to staff what aspects of their work they are doing well, what aspects need improvement, and how that improvement should occur. Feedback should also leave staff feeling encouraged about their work.

# Protocol for Giving Feedback to Improve Staff Performance

Here is a way of giving feedback based on observed work performance that has been shown to be effective in improving staff work and to be well accepted by staff.

- *Component 1:* Begin the feedback session by saying something positive about the observed performance. The reason for beginning with something positive is to make the feedback session more pleasant for staff. Also, by beginning with a positive statement, any worry or anxiety staff may feel about having had their work observed can be reduced.

- *Component 2:* Tell the staff what they did correctly or skillfully during the observation. The comments to staff should be very specific, such as "The way you helped him fold the towel with a verbal prompt was great!" not something more general like "Good job".

- *Components 3 and 4:* Tell staff what they did wrong (if applicable) and how they could improve their performance.

- *Component 5:* Prompt staff to ask questions to ensure that they heard and understood what you have told them about their performance.

- *Component 6:* Tell staff when the next observation will be conducted. Telling staff when the next observation will be conducted shows that your attention to the skills being observed will continue. Staff are more likely to pay attention to the feedback and adjust their performance if they know you will continue to look at their work. Information provided about when the next observation will occur may either be specific (e.g., next Monday during breakfast) or general (e.g., during the next week).

- *Component 7:* Make sure that the last thing said to staff concerning the observed performance is positive or encouraging. In other words, *end the session on an upbeat note.* Ending with a positive statement will help staff feel better about the feedback and encouraged about their work.

# Module 22: Performance Checklists

**Objectives:**

Upon completion of this module, trainees should be able to:
(1) Describe a checklist as a task analysis of a staff work duty
(2) Discuss what kinds of work duties are monitored with
     checklists
(3) Name at least two advantages of using a checklist
(4) Create a simple checklist for observing a job duty within
     the trainee's agency

## What Is a Performance Checklist?

A primary part of a supervisor's job is to make sure staff know
what is expected of them in terms of their work duties. One tool
that can help inform staff about a specific job duty, and make it
easier for a supervisor to observe and evaluate how well staff
perform the duty, is a performance checklist.

---

> A *performance checklist* is simply a task analysis
> of a staff work duty in which all the steps
> for completing the duty are listed.

---

When observing staff performance using a checklist, each step
on the checklist can be marked by the supervisor as correct or
incorrect as the step is completed by the staff member.

A checklist can also be used to monitor the outcome of a staff member's work. Here is an example of a checklist for observing one type of outcome of staff work.

---

**Checklist for Writing a Progress Note**

*NA = Not Applicable*

1. Entry into record is dated    **Yes No**

2. Current level of performance is
stated for each target skill    **Yes No**

3. Current performance is compared
to previous performance indicating
whether or not progress has occurred
on each target skill    **Yes No**

4. If no progress has occurred in three
months, action for addressing the
lack of progress is specified   **Yes No NA**

5. Entry in record is signed    **Yes No**

---

As a supervisor reviews a staff member's progress note, the supervisor can check to see if each item is included in the progress note. This checklist does not illustrate the only way to write a progress note, just one way that was required in a particular agency.

# When a Checklist Is Useful

- Checklists are useful for observing work duties that are complex. Complex work duties require staff to perform several different actions to successfully complete the duty.

For example, a Behavior Support Plan (BSP) may require staff to do several specific things when a person they support appears angry in order to prevent the person from hurting someone. These steps could be listed in a checklist. The checklist could be used by the supervisor to observe each staff's interaction with the person when the person is angry to make sure the BSP is carried out correctly.

- When a work duty must be observed from beginning to end to get an accurate evaluation of a staff member's performance, a checklist is usually a helpful monitoring tool.

For example, a supervisor must observe from the time a teaching interaction begins until the teaching interaction is complete to determine if staff are teaching correctly. A checklist including each of the steps of the task analysis that indicates whether prompts, reinforcement, and error correction for each step are applied correctly could be helpful in evaluating a staff member's teaching skills.

- When work duties require exactness and are important for staff to do in a specific way, checklists may be helpful.

Keeping the appropriate documentation when a person we support has an accident or injury is important for several reasons, including legal requirements. The types of documentation required when a person has an accident or injury can be included on a checklist so staff know exactly what must be documented. This type of checklist would also be helpful to supervisors who must review the documentation to make sure staff have documented everything that is supposed to be documented.

## Advantages of Using a Checklist

- A checklist reminds the supervisor to look for important actions.

- A checklist makes it easy to give the right feedback to staff. After an observation is complete, the supervisor can simply glance at the checklist to know what staff did correctly and incorrectly.

- After a supervisor gives staff verbal feedback based on a checklist, the checklist can be given to staff. When staff look at the checklist at a later time, it reminds them how the work should be done.

- A checklist helps supervisors to observe consistently. When the same checklist is used each time a work duty is observed, a supervisor can tell if staff are improving by comparing the number of steps performed correctly on a current checklist with the number of steps performed correctly on previous checklists.

# Module 23: Staff Observation

**Objectives:**                                    **Trainee Notes**

Upon completion of this module, trainees should be
    able to:

(1) Describe four guidelines for obtaining information
    about staff performance
(2) Conduct an observation in a manner that is likely to
    be acceptable to staff

## A Supervisor's Primary Job

The primary job of a supervisor is to make sure the
quality of staff work is good enough to provide the
support needed by the people with developmental
disabilities that the agency serves. When staff work is
not good enough, a supervisor's job is to make
improvements. When staff work is good, a supervisor's
job is to maintain staff work performance. Maintaining
means ensuring that staff continue to do good work.

In order for supervisors to know what parts of a staff
member's work to improve and what parts to maintain
(e.g., what to give feedback about), supervisors must
know how well staff perform all important job duties.
For the next few minutes, we will discuss how a
supervisor should get information about staff
performance.

---

**Guidelines for Getting Information About Staff Work**

Get first-hand information by directly observing
staff work or outcomes of staff work.

Gather information in a consistent manner.

Observe staff performance frequently.

Make observation as pleasant as possible for staff.

---

# Rely on First-Hand Information

Supervisors should rely on first-hand information when
evaluating staff work. First-hand means that supervisors
should directly *observe* staff work. For example, if a
supervisor is concerned about how a staff member
interacts with supported workers at a job site, the
supervisor should visit the site to observe the staff
member's interactions.

Another good way for supervisors to get first-hand
information about staff work is by observing the
outcomes of staff work. For example, if a supervisor
wants to know if staff are providing the right adaptive
equipment at mealtime, the supervisor can observe
sometime during a meal to see if people with disabilities
have the right equipment.

Supervisors should not form opinions about staff work based on reports from other staff members or co-workers. Other staff may have different expectations or may not be familiar enough with the work situation to fairly judge a staff person's work. Sometimes, other staff are jealous of, or angry with, a staff member so they describe that person's work in a negative way.

Again, the best way to gather information about staff work is to directly observe staff at work or observe the outcomes or products of staff work.

## Be Consistent in Getting Information

A second guideline is to get information about staff work in a consistent way. That is, each time a particular work activity is observed, the way the work is observed should be the same.

Unless we observe important job duties in the same way each time, changes noted in staff performance may only be the result of how the job duty was observed and not any real change in the staff person's actual performance. When staff observations are conducted *in*consistently, supervisors will not know if their supervisory efforts to improve or maintain staff performance are having the desired effect.

For example, suppose you have conducted training to improve staff interactions with the people they support. Without a consistent way to observe the quality of staff interactions both before and after the training, your opinion of how well staff are interacting may vary. Your opinion could be influenced by the mood you are in, your relationship with a particular staff member, or other events that have happened before an observation. It will be hard to tell if training has made a difference in how staff interact.

During this training, several observation tools for evaluating different areas of staff performance have been discussed. These include the:

• Teaching Skills Checklist

• Group Interaction Observation Form

• Checklist for Giving Choices

These types of observation tools help supervisors to observe staff performance the same way each time an observation is conducted. We have also talked about how to create these types of checklists to consistently evaluate other important job duties required of staff.

## Make Frequent Observations

Staff work should be observed frequently. Frequent observations give supervisors a more accurate picture of a staff member's performance. If supervisors observe staff only on rare occasions, the good (or bad) impression supervisors get may not reflect the staff member's usual way of working. Also, when supervisors observe frequently, staff are less likely to be anxious when observed because observation becomes a part of the normal routine.

When staff are observed directly, consistently, and frequently, staff are more likely to think evaluations of their work are fair.


## Make Observations Acceptable

As just discussed, observations are necessary to make sure staff are doing their jobs the right way. Supervisors informally observe what staff are doing whenever they come into the work area during the normal routine. Informal observations usually do not cause staff to feel uncomfortable because the observations occur as part of the supervisor's ongoing duties.

However, when observations are more formal, such as those using checklists or other monitoring forms, staff almost always report that they dislike having their work monitored.   To make everyone's job (including the supervisor's) more enjoyable, formal observations should be conducted in ways that make observations as pleasant as possible for staff.

The way supervisors conduct observations can make staff feel comfortable or uncomfortable.   When observations are more pleasant, they will be more acceptable to staff. One good way to make observations acceptable to staff is to use the following guidelines when conducting a formal observation.

- Greet the staff member in a pleasant manner when you arrive in the work area to observe.

- Explain the reason for the observation.  Staff should be familiar with any observation form that is routinely used to monitor their performance. Being familiar with the observation process makes it more comfortable for staff.

- Use common sense regarding when to observe. Do not conduct formal observations during unusual situations such as when a person with a disability is extremely upset or when a staff member needs help to handle a situation. At times like these, supervisors need to help in some way.

- Give feedback immediately after the observation. We have already discussed how to provide feedback.

- Thank the staff member for participating in the observation before leaving the work area.

# Module 24: Training Staff

## Objectives:

Upon completion of this module, trainees should be able to:

(1) Describe the importance of staff training as part of a supervisor's job
(2) Demonstrate steps of performance- and competency-based staff training

## Training Staff as A Part of A Supervisor's Job

A key part of positive behavior support is training staff in the values, goals, and procedures of positive behavior support. Training staff in positive behavior support can occur in different ways. It can be done by training with this curriculum as you have been experiencing. It can also be done by clinicians and others with behavioral skills, such as people who develop behavior support plans (BSPs).

However, the most important resource for training staff in positive behavior support and other job skills is the staff *supervisor*. Supervisors are usually the most knowledgeable people about what support staff are supposed to do as well as their day-to-day job situations. Staff also usually turn to their supervisors when they are not sure how to do something on the job.

143

In short, training staff is a critical part of every supervisor's job.

In this class we will describe an evidence-based way supervisors can train staff. We will focus on training staff to carry out BSPs as part of positive behavior support. However, the same training approach can be used to train essentially any important job skill to staff. The training process we will discuss is known as *performance-* and *competency-based staff training.* More recently it has also become known as *behavioral skills training.*

Performance- and competency-based training consists of staff trainers carrying out the following steps.

- **Describe to staff how to do the skill.** The description of what staff are expected to do should include a rationale for why the skill being trained to staff is important.

- **Give staff a written description of how to do the skill**. The written description is something staff can look at later to remind them how to do the skill. For example, when training staff to follow a BSP, staff should be given a copy of the plan to read. If the BSP is very long, only the parts describing what staff are to do can be given to staff.

- **Show (model) the skill.** Too often, staff training consists of only the steps mentioned so far. That is, when training staff to follow BSPs, staff are told what to do and are perhaps given a copy of the written plan. Typically, these two steps alone are not enough. Staff are more likely to learn to carry out the plan correctly if they are also shown how to do the main parts of the plan.

- **Observe as staff practice the skill and give positive and corrective feedback.** Remember to give feedback following the 7-step protocol we talked about in a previous module.

- **Repeat modeling, observation, and staff practice with feedback until staff do the skill the right way.** Depending on the skill being trained, it may take many demonstrations by the supervisor followed by staff practice before the skill is learned. When BSPs contain a number of procedures for decreasing problem behaviors and increasing replacement behaviors, for example, several training sessions involving practice with feedback may be needed.

# Simulated Training
# Versus Training at the Work Site

When first training staff to do a new skill, training can be done in simulation. Training in simulation can be done in a classroom away from the people we support using role-play techniques. The role-play and practice activities we have done during these classes are examples of training in simulation.

It is often necessary to train many skills for providing positive behavior support in simulation at first. This is likely to include training in how to deal with problem behaviors and new or complex task analyses for teaching a new skill.

Simulation training is necessary because behavior problems may occur infrequently, making it difficult for staff to get enough on-the-job practice to learn how to deal with behavior problems. Also, in many cases, we do not know when behavior problems will occur. Supervisors cannot plan staff training sessions to take place exactly when the problem behavior occurs.

Another reason for beginning BSP implementation training in simulation is to ensure the safety and dignity of the person being supported. For example, if a "prompted re-dressing" procedure is implemented when a person removes his/her clothing in a non-private location, staff should be as skillful as possible *before* prompting the person to put clothes back on so the person is treated with respect. Staff should practice the prompting re-dressing procedure in simulation before using the procedure with anybody.

Once staff have mastered a skill in simulation, we must then observe staff use the skill during the regular job. Remember that we cannot be sure staff can perform a skill in the actual work setting until they demonstrate the skill in the work setting. For example, if staff have been taught to use a "prompted re-dressing" procedure in simulation, supervisors must see staff correctly use the procedure on the job before considering staff training completed.

---

**An important rule in staff training:**

Staff training is not complete until staff demonstrate
they can do the skill in the work setting.

---

Performance- and competency-based training has been
used to teach almost all of the performance skills
covered during these classes.  Think about it . . .

- First, we described each skill.

- Second, we provided written information in
  handouts and on the slide projector.

- Third, we demonstrated each skill.

- Fourth, you practiced the skills with feedback
  from either a trainer or other trainees.

The importance of seeing the skill demonstrated in the
actual work site has not been overlooked in this training.
Each of you either has been or will be required to
demonstrate some of the most important skills covered
during this training at your work site.

# Formal versus Informal Staff Training

Staff training does not always have to be a preplanned and formal process. In fact, one of the most important jobs of a supervisor is to provide staff training as needed and on a routine basis whenever the supervisor observes staff work.

When staff training occurs informally, the steps are basically the same ones we have already discussed for use in more formal staff training. The supervisors should: 1) describe the skill, 2) model the right way to do the skill, 3) observe staff practice the skill, and 4) give feedback until the staff person does the skill correctly.

# Module 25: Performance Analysis

## Objectives:

Upon completion of this module trainees should be able to:

(1) Describe the steps supervisors should take when staff do not know how to carry out a BSP
(2) Describe the steps supervisors should take when staff know how to carry out the BSP but do not carry it out
(3) Describe what supervisors should do when staff show improvement in carrying out a BSP after receiving feedback
(4) Describe what supervisors should do when staff show no improvement in carrying out a BSP after receiving feedback
(5) Develop a plan for making on-the-job improvements in positive behavior support

━━━━━◀ ◆ ◀◆▶━━━━━

## Reasons Why Behavior Support Plans May Not Work

In a previous class, we discussed three primary reasons why a Behavior Support Plan (BSP) may not be effective. The main reasons include:

- Plans are not carried out when they should be carried out

- Plans are not carried out in the way the plans are written

- Plans do not have what is needed to help a person we support overcome a problem behavior

We have also discussed the importance of frequently observing staff carrying out a BSP to determine which of the reasons just mentioned might be responsible when the BSP is not working. If observations indicate that staff are not carrying out the plan, or are not carrying out parts of the plan correctly, the supervisor must take action to see that staff carry out the plan as written.

The purpose of this module is to discuss the actions supervisors can take to help staff carry out BSPs. We will discuss the most common situations in which a BSP is not working and what supervisors should do in each situation.

**Staff do not carry out a BSP because they do not know how to carry it out...**

**Supervisory Action:  Provide staff training**

Performance- and competency-based staff training is one of the best ways to train staff to carry out BSPs. This approach to staff training was discussed in detail earlier in this training. At this point, we will briefly review the steps of performance- and competency-based staff training.

**Training Step 1:  Describe to staff what to do to carry out the BSP.** Supervisors should tell staff what to do to implement each major part of the BSP, including how to:

- set up the environment to prevent problem behavior

- respond to antecedents that usually occur before the problem behavior

- respond to target behaviors to be increased

- respond to target behaviors to be decreased

**Training Step 2:  Give staff a written description of what to do**.  When staff have questions about what they should do and the supervisor is not available, they can refer to the written information to remind them what to do.

**Training Step 3: Show staff what to do by modeling how to carry out the BSP**.  Demonstrating how to carry out the BSP means that *supervisors* must know how to carry out all parts of the BSP.  If supervisors are unsure of how to carry out all parts of the plan, they should contact the support team member who wrote the plan to get training for themselves.

**Training Step 4:  Have staff practice carrying out the BSP while the supervisor watches and gives positive and corrective feedback.**

In a previous class we talked about a way to give effective and acceptable feedback.  To briefly review, we give feedback by:

- Beginning the feedback session by saying something positive to staff

- Telling staff what they did right with specific details

- Telling staff what they did wrong and specifically what they should have done to carry out the plan correctly

- Asking staff if they have any questions concerning the feedback

- Telling staff when the next observation will occur

- Ending with a positive statement about staff performance

**Training Step 5: Repeat modeling and feedback with practice until the staff person can correctly carry out the BSP**. You cannot be sure staff know how to carry out the BSP until you see them do it right. Remember that it may take many practice sessions with feedback before staff learn to correctly carry out all parts of a BSP. However, supervisors should expect to see improvement in how well staff carry out the plan after each feedback session.

Once staff are trained to carry out the plan and you have seen them carry out the plan correctly, then you know that they have the skills they need to carry out the plan on a routine basis.

**Staff know how to carry out the plan but do not carry out the plan...**

**Supervisor action: Provide feedback**

If staff know how to carry out the plan but observations indicate that the plan is still not being carried out, the supervisor should give staff additional feedback. Again, the feedback should follow the basic protocol previously described.

**Staff carry out the BSP or carry out the BSP <u>better</u> after receiving feedback...**

**Supervisor action: Provide positive feedback or other positive consequences to encourage more good work**

An important part of a supervisor's job is to motivate staff to continue to do good work. The positive consequences that a supervisor provides depends on what is important and valued by a particular staff member and, also, what is acceptable practice within a given agency.

**Staff do not carry out the plan despite feedback...**

**Supervisor action: Begin disciplinary action**

When staff members do not show improvement in carrying out the BSP after several sessions of feedback, the staff person's performance should be discussed with the supervisor's supervisor for additional guidance. If disciplinary action is required, the action should be taken according to the agency's personnel policy.

Although disciplinary action is not a pleasant thing to do, it is necessary when staff do not improve with supervisory feedback. The goals of positive behavior support are to help people we support live as independently and enjoyably as possible. When staff members do not carry out BSPs as written, they are harming the progress and well-being of people with disabilities.

These staff members must improve their work if they are to continue working in the agency.

**Staff members are carrying out the BSP as written but identified behaviors are not getting better**

**Supervisor action: Get help to change the BSP**

If the supervisor has taken the necessary action to ensure that staff are carrying out the BSP as it is written and – after a reasonable amount of time – the behavior of concern is not getting better, the plan must be brought to the attention of the support team to decide how the plan should be changed.

## Develop A Plan for Improving Positive Behavior Support on The Job

In this series of classes, we have discussed many areas of staff performance that might affect the quality of an agency's positive behavior support. For example, we have discussed the importance of staff interacting positively with the people they support, selecting functional skills to teach, effectively teaching new skills, providing choices, and implementing specific BSPs for individuals they support.

Supervisors can improve the performance of individuals or groups of staff members in any of these areas using the supervision strategies we have also discussed in these classes.

The last activity for this series of classes is to work together with other people from your agency to develop a plan for improving some aspect of positive behavior support within your agency. During the activity you should decide what skills learned in the course will be most useful in your agency, the obstacles likely to make it hard to implement the skills and finally, an outline of a plan for improving aspects of positive behavior support in your agency. The course trainers will lead you through each of these steps.